PLOT 29

Allan Jenkins

PLOT 29

a memoir

4th ESTATE · *London*

HarperCollins
PUBLISHERS
Since 1817

4th Estate
An imprint of HarperCollins*Publishers*
1 London Bridge Street
London SE1 9GF
www.4thEstate.co.uk

First published in Great Britain by 4th Estate in 2017

1 3 5 7 9 8 6 4 2

Copyright © Allan Jenkins 2017
Except Foreword copyright © Nigel Slater 2017

The right of Allan Jenkins to be identified as the author
of this work has been asserted by him in accordance
with the Copyright, Design and Patents Act 1988

This book is based on the author's experiences. Some names,
identifying characteristics, dialogue and details have been
changed, reconstructed or fictionalised.

A catalogue record for this book is
available from the British Library

ISBN 978-0-00-812196-9

Printed and bound in Great Britain by
Clays Ltd, St Ives plc

MIX
Paper from
responsible sources
FSC® C007454

FSC™ is a non-profit international organisation established to promote
the responsible management of the world's forests. Products carrying the
FSC label are independently certified to assure consumers that they come
from forests that are managed to meet the social, economic and
ecological needs of present and future generations,
and other controlled sources.

Find out more about HarperCollins and the environment at
www.harpercollins.co.uk/green

For Christopher

FOREWORD

There are two sorts of gardeners, those who inherit a plot of land and cover it with a lawn, a neatly manicured patch of grass to trim and mow in straight lines for all to admire. Others use their space to grow, nurture and share. They dig deep, they replenish the soil, plant seed and watch it grow. They protect and nurture what lives there, and then they share the bounty.

You can go about writing a memoir in two ways too. You can pen a story that plasters over the cracks, telling tales of heroism and success. Or you can break ground, dig deeper, bravely unearthing an altogether richer story. One that takes its author and its readers down a track that is by turns surprising, tender and, occasionally, unsettling.

I have never read anything quite like *Plot 29*. Yes, it's the gentle, heart-warming tale of the rescue and repair of an abandoned allotment, of protection offered to the soil by someone who understands the joys and pitfalls of growing. But contained in these pages is also an extra-ordinary memoir, brave, exquisitely written and utterly compelling.

Nigel Slater, 2017

NATURE

When I am disturbed, even angry, gardening is a therapy. When I don't want to talk, I turn to Plot 29 or to a wilder piece of land by a northern sea. There among seeds and trees my breathing slows, my heart rate too. My anxieties slip away.

It's not always like that. Sometimes I just want to grow potatoes surrounded by flowers, like I did aged five with my brother one magical summer with our new mum and dad.

Plot 29 is on a London allotment site where people come together to grow. It's just that sometimes what I am growing along with marigolds and sorrel is solace. I nurture small plants from seed like when I was small and needed someone to care for me. I offer protection from predators like when I tried to guard Christopher.

This then is my journal and childhood memoir, though my memories are fractured like my family. So I immerse myself in the plot, in nature and nurture. I lose myself in rapture. I grow fresh peas for my peace of mind.

It's not all about healing, of course, though it's there in abundance like beans. Sometimes it is the simple joy of growing food and flowers and sharing with people you love.

CAST LIST

Allotment family
Mary, Howard, Annie, Bill, Jeffrey, John, Ruth

Family
Henriette... ... ... wife
Christopher, Lesley, Caron, Susan,
Michael, Mandy, Adeboye, Tina ... brothers and sisters
Lilian and Dudley ... ... mum and dad
Sheila ... ... mother
Ray   ... ... father
Billy and Doris ... ... grandparents
Terry, Tony, Colin, Mike, Joyce   ... uncles and aunt
Allan, Alan, Peter ... ... me

PLOT 29

By God, the old man could handle a spade.
Just like his old man.

Seamus Heaney, *Digging*

JUNE

It is the month of early visits, of waking before 5am when the plot calls. The time of growth and hazel wigwams. Time to be concerned about seed. I lie awake – or sit at work – imagining the tender seedlings at the mercy of wind, rain, sun, slugs. Will they make it through infancy? With my help, maybe.

By 6am I am at the allotment, the air soft, the light too, the robin, maybe the fox, my only companions. The baby beans, only two leaves tall, are vulnerable now. Will they make it past the snails lying in wait like bullies? Within two weeks they will be free, snaking up hazel poles in a speeded-up film. Next month they'll be two metres high, stems entwined, feeling for the next stick like rock climbers on a difficult face. Flowers will start to grow, pods begin to form. But for now I stand on the sidelines, a parent on sports day, calling urgent encouragement. Soon, like kids, they will be old enough to fend for themselves but for now at least I am here, not so much to do anything – the bed is hoed, weeded, pretty pristine – but as a friend, odd as this sounds, so they know they are not alone.

I learned, I think, to love from seed, much as other kids had puppies, kittens, fluffy toys. But it was the hopeful helplessness of seed that called, something vulnerable to care for. The urge to protect, to be there, was strong, like I couldn't be for my brother Christopher when I left him alone in the children's home; for my sister Lesley, out of harm's way, I thought, with her dad, or Caron, whom my mother would abandon while she searched for new men, new sex, excitement.

SATURDAY 6 AM. Sunlight has not yet hit the plot. Bill is sleeping less well since his wife died, so he comes here to kill time until Costa Coffee opens at 8am and he meets with his fellow insomniacs. His is the tidiest plot, mani-cured almost, everything neat in formal rows, plants perfectly spaced, celery blanching in brown paper, runner beans climbing up curly wire, blackcurrant bushes shrouded by nets. His seedlings are grown at home and transplanted into regimented rills. It wouldn't work for me. I obsessively grow from seed *in situ*, needing the magical moment when an anxious scan along a row is rewarded by broken soil, a tiny stem breaking through like a baby turtle released from the egg before its dash to the sea. It has been two weeks since I have been here, and the salads have overgrown. Rows of rocket flowers shaped like ships' propellers, land cress crowned with yellow spikes. The beans are under siege from slugs. Many inch-high stems are decimated, stunted, the baby-turtle equivalent of gulls swooping yards from the shore. Some have been simply obliterated. There is a sappy, fast growth to much of the plant life, perfect for predatory snails. Something has stripped a broad bean pod, though there are still many left. I walk through dew-soaked leaves and throw a few slugs over the wall. I will return later to pull much of the salad and let light in on the denser growth but the afternoon plan is to clear more of Mary's beds.

Plot 29 belongs to Mary Wood, who has shared it with my friend Howard Sooley and me since 2009, when Don, her husband, died. Not because she couldn't cope with the space (she is a gifted gardener) but because it produces more food, she says, than she can eat. Mary is poorly at the moment. As her energy levels have dropped, the weeds, the wild, have pressed in, strangling the plot. I am here to clear her green manure. Narcotised bees are everywhere, seemingly overdosing on nectar. They fall stoned to the soil as I clear. Sycamore seedlings infest the bed, the overwintered chard is blown, a metre tall, menacing nettles taller. I work quickly, scything, clearing, restoring order. It feels important now that Mary's plot doesn't also succumb to attack.

I clear the bed, transplanting a couple of short rows of six-inch chards, sowing another of beetroot seed. I return later to talk to her. She is here less than in previous years but sunshine and a need to replant sweet peas has drawn her out. She has a chair on the allotment now, and sits more often. We talk about what she wants to grow this year, and where. I cut pea sticks for a row at the bottom of the bed. With little time to work our part of the plot, I sow nasturtium on the border.

My gardening life, in some ways my life, begins with this simple seed. Most of my memories start at the age of five, perhaps because there are photos from then, perhaps because almost everything before then was chaos to be peeled away later in the therapist's chair and in talks with members of my 'birth family' (a sly phrase we have been taught to say instead of 'real'), when I found them many years later. Perhaps simply because that is where safety starts. With Lilian and Dudley Drabble.

There is a photo of my brother Christopher and me with Lilian as young boys. Christopher is lopsidedly smiling, proudly holding his new ginger kitten. It almost matches his hair. Lilian is crouched with Tonka, her Siamese cat. I have my arm around her, looking a little warily into the camera. The boys' clothes are comically big. Not 'you will grow into them' big, but clothes bought while the intended children aren't (have never been) there. We were small for our age. But these are new clothes for a new life in our new home with our new family.

Lilian and Dudley married in their forties. They met when she nursed his dying father. Too old to have children, they at first looked to adopt a baby girl but were denied, perhaps because of age. It was a loss Lilian would always feel. She wanted someone all her own, someone she could mould and make, who would wear dresses. There was somehow always a sadness we couldn't assuage.

Meanwhile, the Drabbles offered respite to 'damaged' children at their picture-postcard post office on Dartmoor. Christopher and I spent a weekend there, shooting bows and arrows, learning to say please and thank you (we were 'guttural' Dudley would later delight in telling me).

Plymouth children's homes were feral then. Snarling packs sniffing out fears, tears, blood. Not always only the boys.

We learned a lesson about caste here. First, of course, there were the Brahmins: the 'Famous Five' families with their normal 'mum and dad' (small words still able, occasionally, to conjure black holes of unhappiness).

The adopted were the 'chosen ones', mostly children of the over-fertile underclass taken in by the infertile middle class. The unworthy become worthy, if you will; a shift in status almost impossible to imagine – a parole from purgatory.

Foster families were holding pens – a sifting, shifting, near-family life spent waiting. Here we would practise being appreciative and loving, living under the fear or hope or threat of the knock on the door. A dread visit from the social worker, who might pass you along, around or back.

At the bottom, of course, the untouchable unlovables. The broken kids in care with the mark of Cain, the ones no one wants. My brother Christopher.

Residential care operated like dogs' homes – abandoned pets kept penned until someone, anyone, might take them. I remember days my hair was specially brushed. I was told to smile, because new parents might see me, heal me, love me, take me off the city's hands. There is a skill, you see, to being lovable: a fluffy, undamaged Disney dog, eager to engage, with a wagging tail. Christopher couldn't or wouldn't learn. People were nervous of his nervous tic. His face twitched, his mouth twisted. He was stunted. The runt of the litter with perhaps a subtle hint of trouble to come. Though appearances can be deceptive.

I was rehomed but would keen for Christopher until they returned me to the pack, just another ungrateful, undeserving boy. Until the days of Lilian and Dudley Drabble, their house on a Devon river, a kitten, a cat and a magic packet of nasturtium seed.

I grow it still, this unruly, gaudy flower. It is prone to infestation, the first to fall over in the frost, but my gardening is saturated in emotional memories, as with music and love. So I sow nasturtiums because they are tangled up like bindweed with thoughts of the boy I was, the boy I became, the brother I lost, perhaps the father I'll never know. And I sow runner beans for Mary because Don, her late husband, grew them. Mary also offered me a home, a place to grow when I didn't have one. So we talk about peas and radishes, about the rocket and lettuce I will sow when she starts treatment.

Later in the week, I meet with Howard to stir biodynamic cow manure by hand in water for an hour. From the beginning of working the allotment we chose to work this way, inspired by Jane Scotter of Fern Verrow farm in Herefordshire, the finest grower we know. In most areas of my life I carefully calculate risk and reward, working within tight budgets and remits. Here, it is different; organic plants grow, foxes are free, flowers spread, children run around. As an adolescent I was banned from confirmation class for being unable to buy into the church, the resurrection and miracles but I have since learned to suspend my disbelief. A journalist, I stop asking questions and try to listen. We follow a lunar planting calendar and avoid invasive pest control. We believe our crops last longer, taste better – the rocket is hotter, the beetroot sweeter, the sorrel more sour. It works for us. We feel more connected to the soil. It suits us and the space.

There is something deeply meditative about the stirring process, encouraging you to focus, to sit still for an hour at dusk or dawn, whatever the weather. Howard has to leave early, so I also spray the mix around Mary's plot.

The next morning I am at the allotment early to sow rows for Mary and me. I am keen to catch up. I was exiled from the plot with a fractured ankle for four months over the winter. There was a disconnect from the soil with which my wellbeing is intricately entwined. Suddenly, catastrophically, walking and gardening, the twin chemical-free medications I have built into my life, were shattered along with my bones. I am rebuilding this connection now, but it is slow. I am back walking along the canal to work, over the heath or along beaches, but I have missed the overwinter planting that greens the brown soil that surrounds us. I have a thought the plot is sulking, like a cat or child that has been left alone too long. The three bean structures I have built on the two plots are prone to attack. The urge for organic slug pellets is strong.

Later, an allotment neighbour comes to talk over bad news. William, the kindly chairman of the association, has been found dead in his flat. I have always been grateful to him for the gentle way he defused tension between the plot holders and the helpers. William had been forced to leave his native South Africa when his student activism had come to the attention of the Afrikaans authorities. In London, he had written and directed successful plays, he had been a book reviewer, pictures showed he had been beautiful, but the William I knew was a shy, bespectacled man who grew tulips and peonies, and at whose plot I always stopped to talk about gardening, the weather and the problems with sharing sheds.

The slugs may be winning their battle with the climbing beans. The early salads have bolted. The garlic and shallots that had looked green and healthy only a few days ago have succumbed to papery rust and need to be pulled. The wild Tuscan calendula has spread like duckweed and is smothering other plants. For my first time in June, the plot is in need of a reboot. The living carpet that normally covers the soil is threadbare and worn. A couple of weeks before midsummer I start again. It is hard sometimes not to think that your garden says something about you, the green fingers you hope you have, your innate ability (or inability) to nurture. Hard not to feel good about yourself when the plot thrives, or like a failure when it falls. The fault must be yours and not the seed, the weather or blight on the site.

Without early success at growing as a kid, I guess, I might not be doing it now. It was the first time as a child I thought I might be gifted at something. In south Devon, Dudley gave Christopher and me two pocket-sized patches of garden and two packets of seed. Christopher had African marigolds (tagetes): bright orange, cheery, the stuff of temple garlands. I was handed nasturtium flowers: chaotic cascades of reds, oranges and yellows (Dad liked bright colours), which soon overflowed. Caper-shaped seed heads would dry in the sun. I was amazed (still am) that so much life can come from a small packet. Later my nasturtiums would fall prey to black fly, a nightmare infestation sucking sugary life. Lilian showed me how to spray leaves and stems with soapy water, holding back the devastation until frost would turn their green into limp, ghostly grey; a silvery sheen of dew signalling the end. I would pull them, shake out seed for next year (though the self-seeding was always enough) and throw the lifeless bodies on the compost pile to rot down and turn into soil. This idea of nature's renewal fascinated me. I was in love.

For the first few years at the allotment I helped with a primary school's gardening club, where children from five to 11 learned to grow. Kids who might be having trouble settling in class worked together during Friday lunchtimes. Seedlings grown in the greenhouse were replanted in raised beds in the playground. I would host their visits to the site. Branch Hill, where we are, is like a Victorian secret garden: gated, only just domesticated, sheltered by tall trees. We would give the children sunflower seeds and watch them stand, stunned, as the plants grew faster than them. We would eat peas from the pod and taste herbs. One memory sticks: watching the blossoming of a Somali-born girl. At first head down and standing shyly at the back of the group, she began to join in, to enquire about sorrel, lovage and other flavours unfamiliar to her. By the end of the year, impatient at the gate, she would rush to ask for magic nasturtium, her favourite 'spicy flower'.

1960. Christopher is morphing from an undersized child into a fast-growing boy. The nervous reserve is fading too. He is talking more often, more excitedly. Always out with his fishing rod or digging for bait. I don't have the stomach for threading anxious ragworm on to a hook. We never eat fish he has caught. He never brings it home.

He doesn't like fish for tea anyway. He is a meat and potato boy. His favourite: Heinz spaghetti on toast. He gradually drifts towards the village. He can more clearly hear its call: the dog whistle of other kids. I see them on the hills, on the horizon, like spotting a fox. Within a few years he is a natural athlete, gifted at sport. He is better at being a boy than me. He is more natural. Cars and bikes, cricket and football; later, beer with bigger lads. Soon after we arrive, Dudley builds us a push cart. He paints it bright yellow and blue. Chris's freckled face brightens as we tear down the hill behind the house, laughing as we hurtle towards the river, skewing across the tidal road, the wooden handbrake screaming as we mostly avoid the mud. He is gradually healing from his fear. He is gaining height and weight. After a few years of living in Aveton Gifford he is an annoying inch taller than me.

I am back at the plot and the snails are still rampant on Mary's patch. I am not sure why. I have cleared a lot of weed and there are few secret places left to hide. Maybe it is just their year. I have sown and re-sown peas and beans but they cull the baby shoots almost every time. Skeletal seedlings lie at the base of the poles. It's a bean battlefield. I succumb, finally, to buying organic pellets. The biodynamic thought-police would frown but I cannot have thriving crops while Mary's wigwam is bare. I restock French beans (in three colours: yellow, green and blue) and go up one evening after work. The site is empty, smelling of hay and English summer. Clumps of calendula almost shine through the early gloom. I sow more beans at the base of Mary's poles and uncover the first stirrings of last week's seed, sprouts curled like dormice. I replenish the pea sticks and scatter protective pellets. Time is starting to run out. We are a week from the solstice and I won't be here to help. I am heading to the other magical piece of land in my life, a summerhouse plot on the East Jutland coast, where I plant mostly trees.

It is always odd leaving the allotment for any length of time. I feel as if I am abandoning it and it won't understand. It is a recurring irrational feeling (a theme through my life like a name through seaside rock). But it is stronger now, reinforced by my enforced absence over the winter with broken bones.

The Danish plot is different. It is an echo of Devon. Coastal, even the wide stretch of shallow water and white sand is the same. Here the garden is larger, wilder, more isolated than in London – about 1,500 square metres of sandy loam 300 metres from the sea and a few kilometres from where my 90-year-old Danish mother-in-law lives. Close enough for her to cycle.

We have had this house and land for 10 years now. It is maybe my safest place.

Of course, there are many echoes of Dudley, of our house, Herons Reach, of home. They are here in the climate, in the light, in the anxious dragonflies, the blue butterflies, in the flowers: pink campions in summer, pale primroses in spring – the same shy, unassuming flower I used to pick for Lilian on Mothering Sunday. Here in the finches and tits we feed, in the sudden arrival of migrating flocks that stop off to feast on the wild cherry trees, the red-berried rowan. Here in the orange-backed hares that lope through the meadow, the foxes and badgers that leave tracks in the snow. In the brambles that line the beach, conjuring comforting images of late-summer days, picking through hedges with Lilian, packing small churns with berries, my hands and face stained with juice. Perhaps most of all the memories are in making the blackberry and apple pies that Dudley adored with buttery Devon cream (Lilian was not a gifted cook but she could make a good pie). Yet the deepest Devon echoes are in the trees. Dudley loved to plant trees: poplar and laburnum to line the new drive to the house, Japanese cherry for the autumn-colouring leaf I liked to press between pages of my exercise book; apple (Cox's Orange Pippin for eating, Bramley for cooking), Conference pears and Victoria plums. When I was about seven he planted 200 six-inch Christmas trees it was my job to look after, to trim the choking grass. This was my least favourite chore, worse even than raking the acres of endless lawn. The tiny trees were fiddly, with no hiding place if the shears skipped and a stem was severed. Christopher escaped this because he chopped too many trees. Smart like a fox, my brother.

Perhaps in honour of Dudley, though it is never as explicit as this implies, I grow mostly trees here on Ahl – a few old Danish varieties of apple and plum, three espalier pears, red and blackcurrant bushes, with pine, fir, larch, birch and beech. They are chosen to fit in with the area, a peninsula of old plantations with wooden summerhouses dotted through. When we first found the house, we had to cut down senile trees that surrounded the plot. We chopped them with the help of our neighbours, the same neighbours who gave up weekends to build a shed for the wood they helped saw and split for the stove; the same neighbours who light our morning fire in winter before we arrive. Solitude plus community, the constant I search for, the same as the allotment, an echo of a Devon village life that no longer exists and to which I never belonged.

As with the allotment, I lie wondering about the plot when I am not there, suffering the same wrench when I leave. I sow tulip bulbs in the border in winter with only a slight chance I will see them bloom. The appeal lies in knowing they are part of a dialogue with their surroundings. I am happy if my visits coincide with flowering but I don't have to be here at the time. Finding the spent flowers, petals fallen, their colours faded, is enough. Like the allotment, it is the growing that is the thing. Although I take childish delight in seeing the larch shoot up, reach for the sky, I know I most likely won't see it at its majestic best as a mature tree. But someone will, maybe a small boy as he swings on it or plays in the summer grass. In the meantime I mow, and occasionally remember Dudley carving lawn and meadow and orchard out of field and Devon hill, his beret on (like him, perhaps, a relic from wartime), his neatly trimmed military moustache (ditto), his tightly belted corduroy trousers, grass-green stains on his shoes, and I watch and wait.

I see the larch outstrip the three new birch while its sister tree picks up sunlight and shadow in the other corner. I watch the new, soft green shoots from the saplings bought from an ad in the local paper. I sometimes move the small trees around in the plot until they find their spot and settle. I watch the wild rugosa rose take and spread. The local authority has a love-hate relationship with the sprawling, fragrant flower banks that line the length of the beach, razing them to the ground every year. They are Russian, they say, though the beach has had the roses as long as anyone remembers. The Danes have a conflicted relationship with invasive outsiders, though I, of course, root for the rugosa.

I watch the shy redshanks flutter and feed on ants in the evening. The male calls his morning warning as I pass the bird box they return to every year (I turn left, walking the long way around the house so as not to upset them). I observe the spotted woodpecker train its fledgling in feeding while a tit craftily creeps up behind them in case they miss anything. I listen to the blackbirds as the male sings from the highest branch of the tallest birch and as pairs patrol the lawn, puffed up and important. With these too, I avoid the woodshed when they nest there, a nuisance on cooler Nordic mornings if I want to light a fire.

I admire the starburst of wildflowers on the south side of the house: one year a swooning bank of scarlet poppies, the next year ox-eye daisy, then nothing. I obsessively buy and scatter wild meadow seed to little or no effect. I plant new banks of beech to replace some of the seclusion lost when the tree surgeon ran rampant through the plot. I move the Reine Claude plum to see if it is happier in a slightly shadier spot. Mostly though I train my eye to see the small changes since my last visit: the jewel-coloured beetles, the frogs, the trefoil, the shy hepatica flower, as I lie in the dew for a closer look on my ritual morning walkabout. Everything here is geared towards spring and summer, to the new leaf that shuts out the neighbouring plots, pushes them away, electric green walls if you will, infested with teeming new life, the all-day dawn chorus.

SUNDAY MORNING, LATE JUNE. I am on the first bus, my travelling companions the domestic workers heading to Hampstead, to the larger London homes they clean and care for. I haven't been here for a fortnight and am keen to see the allotment and if the emergency bean sowing has worked. I have missed this place. My heart lifts when I arrive. Mary's bean poles have eager vines on every stick. Her summer plot is saved. OK, tap-rooted thistles are thriving, there is an explosion of weed, many of the peas and broad beans are blown and fallen over, some seed has failed to germinate, but nothing that can't be fixed by a day or two of hand-hoeing. Suddenly, a flash of rust, a glimpse of white on a scurrying tail as a fox darts across my path. My first sighting this summer. A good omen. Maybe omens are a country-kid thing but maybe also the plot will forgive me for my broken leg and absence. I sow saved red tagetes seed and get to work. A break for breakfast at home, a couple of hours for Sunday papers and back to tidy the potatoes. They are close to cropping now. The chard is heavy-leafed and luxuriant. I hoe every row and re-stake the peas in a downpour. I like giving in to gardening in rain. It closes off the outside, focuses your attention. Just you and the job: a meditation of hand and hoe. A moment of connection. I tie the peas and think of a friend who mails me seed. I send him an eclectic collection, saved and shared from around the world, he sends me Basque peas and intense, small tomatoes because they speak of him and his region. The peas are to be picked young, and sometimes when I eat them I remember Ferran Adrià's El Bulli, and I remember Lilian.

2011. It is one of the last nights before the closing of the best restaurant in the world. Dom Perignon has flown in 50 guests by private jet: serious wine investors, Silicon Valley billionaires, film stars, their boyfriends, another food writer and me. We are helicoptered into the beach like a scene from *Apocalypse Now*. We eat 50 small dishes – eggs fashioned from gorgonzola cheese, small, gamy squares of hare, sea cucumber filaments, rose petal wontons and peas. Excited conversation and Dom Perignon '73 flow. I am sitting at a table of high-powered dignitaries when, deep into the meal, a wave hits me. The room and noise fade a little, a shard of emotion breaks free and I notice my face is wet. I am quietly crying. Ferran Adrià's peas have burst in my mouth like memories. I'm no longer sitting opposite Roller Girl from *Boogie Nights*, I am aged maybe six, in shorts and stripy top, on the pink porch of our Devon house. Lilian is there with me, in her yellow patterned summer dress with blue butterfly-wing brooch, sitting, smiling, patiently podding peas into her dented aluminium colander. And as I pick up a pod and help her, I know this is what safety will forever taste like: garden peas freshly picked from the lap of your new mum.

JULY

The broad beans are almost gone now, just a half dozen or so spring-sown Crimson-Flowering from Mads McKeever at Brown Envelope Seed in Cork. I came across this old variety – and Brown Envelope – early in 2007 with the arrival of the Seed Ambassadors. Andrew Still and his wife Sarah are seed hunters from Oregon, where many obsessive plant breeders are based. Andrew's passion is for kale, and the pair were on a European tour starting deep in Siberia and ending with Mads on the west coast of Ireland. With Andrew and Sarah came stories. They arrived at the plot on a cold winter morning with packages: from Tim Peters of Peace Seeds, breeder of Gulag Star, a winter salad cross between Russo-Siberian kales and mustards; our first Flashback Calendula. I learned that day of Trail of Tears beans, named from the winter of 1838 when Cherokee were forced from their farms in the Carolinas and marched to Oklahoma in the Indian Territory. First offered through the American Seed Savers Exchange in 1977 by a 'Cherokee descendent, gardener, seed preservationist, circus owner, and dentist', Dr John Wyche, the beans can now be shared and bought from heirloom growers. I save the seed and still grow the crops Andrew and Sarah gave us. This year, Trail of Tears have made their way on to a couple of Mary's poles to supplement the beans that had been struggling to survive.

The pellets and sun have done their work, the wigwam will thrive this time. I weed around the base, careful not to disturb the geraniums Mary has planted there. Elsewhere, there are ominous signs of smothering bindweed breaking through, but Mary has been clearing another small winter bed. I thin out calendula now rampant on both parts of the plot, the flowers sitting brightly by this screen as I write in the early morning. It is glorious high summer, time to garden with a hat and with the sun on your back, time to harvest lettuces, peas and radishes for home, almost time to sow spinach. But the solstice passed a few weeks ago now, the days are warmer but the nights are a little longer. It's time to begin to plan and plant for winter.

Summer for me is saturated in early memories of Herons Reach, the house on the riverbank that Lilian and Dudley bought to bring up the boys. When I talk of those days, my early life, it is often of 'the boy' (or boys) and what happened to him (or them). I rarely use me or we. It might be to do with confusion or creating a protective distance. I notice other people with a similar background do the same. It might be to do with shedding identity, like the ethereal adder skins I used to find in the Aveton Gifford churchyard. It might be about naming. Mum and Dad didn't like the name Alan, so quickly chose to call me Peter, my middle name, instead. And after a probationary period – I must have passed a test – I was given Drabble (Christopher resisted and stubbornly stuck with

Jenkins, a schism between us). Now that we were safe, they thought we could be safely separated.

Scared city child Alan Jenkins was fading, at least for now. Bright-eyed, blond-haired village boy Peter Drabble was cocooning, being born.

As we played, the house too was being expanded, refashioned and renamed. North Efford (north of the ford), a farm labourer's cottage was metamorphosing into Herons Reach. An extension was added, light was let in, the exterior given a new coat of pink render; rust-red Virginia creeper was trained up its side. That long, happy summer, the first deeply etched into my memory, Dudley waved his phoenix wand, knocking through for French windows, buying the large field behind the house, laying in a drive, the foundations for a lawn, a croft. He planted more trees. Like me, the house was shrugging off its darker past. There was sweet strawberry jam being made in the kitchen, the sound of boys, a cricket bat on ball in the garden, plums and apples were coming in the orchard. Dudley was carving out a home fit for his new family.

While the work was done, we lived in a caravan. It was light, had a breakfast bar and drop-down beds, though we were never inside except to sleep. Christopher would play cricket or football, while I would climb trees and explore the river, catching eels and sticklebacks and putting them in jars until they died.

We had different hair, different eyes, a different smile. He had hazel eyes I almost envied, reddish hair I liked, freckles I wanted, though not the burning in the sun. He was slight while I was heavy, his grin was wider, though mine came more easily.

My favourite photo of Christopher is from that idyllic summer of '59. He is sitting in the doorway of the caravan with a proud-looking Dudley holding him. Christopher is happy – his tic is slowly disappearing. He is being hugged. He is being loved.

The open smile would slowly disappear. His bright, tumbling chatter would go quiet. He would withdraw back into himself, if not quite yet.

JULY 4. We have fruit on all the tomato plants, about a dozen or so, growing in pots on the roof terrace. Ironic they are there, because it is through tomato seed I found Plot 29. It is July 2006, I am editor of a national newspaper Sunday magazine, juggling million-plus budgets, million-plus readership, 20-plus staff. My day is spent dealing with photographers, writers, agents, celebrities and fashion designers with delicate egos. But all I can think of is how my tomato seedlings are faring when the weather changes. How will they cope with the cold or heat? My next *Observer Magazine* cover can wait. I am haunted by helpless plants. For the first time in 20 years, my work has a rival. I feel as if I'm needed elsewhere.

I am not alone. There are a few of us on the magazine currently obsessed. We swap small plants and compare their size. We talk of little else.

I have had a roof terrace at home in Kentish Town for years now where I grow flowers and plants in pots. I am married to a modernist architect who likes clean lines, neat rows of seeding grasses and palms. Every year we compromise on a few geraniums – a hangover from my first teenage job in London at a Kensington garden centre. But the haphazard trays of tomatoes are becoming an issue. Where are they all going to go?

It may be only at work that my obsession is understood. The *Observer Magazine* tomato growers have become competitive. Someone brings their tall seedlings in to show off. We share tomato photographs. And then it hits me: we need a space to grow. Maybe we could sow together, write together, design together, work outside the office. There would be a different dynamic. No one would be the editor, we would create a utopian ideal. We would, I think, grow tomato plants in harmony, like the Diggers or a Sixties collective. I was getting ahead of myself.

We consider guerrilla gardening, transforming urban space. We contact councils to see if they have unused land on a housing estate that would benefit from a few flower and vegetable beds. We ask if there is an empty allotment we could take for a while. Then we find Mary's sister, Hilary, Camden Council's allotment officer, and Branch Hill comes into my life.

2006. Ruth is the tenant of Plot 30. She has waited 18 years for an allotment, until one came along when she wasn't well. It is in north London, near where I live. Hilary says we can garden it for a year and hand it back as a working space. Ruth will hopefully be better by then.

We go to see it.

Ruth's plot neighbours the one we garden now. My first allotment love, it is hard to make out at the start, not so much overgrown as swamped with weed. It falls quickly away down a steep slope, littered with bindweed, bushes, large abandoned lumps of concrete. This is allotment as waste land. My companions' faces fall. Mine lights up. Here is territory I have long understood: a garden damsel in distress; beautiful, abandoned, like a rundown river cottage that needs work and a helping hand to express itself.

It starts well. Magazine staff give up weekends to dig. We are seeing ourselves in a different light: muddy, more than a little sweat. But there is too much to do. It will take too long. The weeds are endemic and we are digging out lumps of old buildings lurking malevolently underground. We unearth an Anderson bomb shelter complete with corrugated roof. It is too much to ask. It is their weekend, time to get away from work. Within a few weeks I am on my own, with the rain, the buried bricks, the wire and broken glass for company. Enter Howard and Don and Mary.

I'd first hired Howard to take photographs for Monty Don's gardening column in the magazine and had loved his work since seeing his book with Derek Jarman on the Prospect Cottage garden in Dungeness. This was austere, artful planting in almost savage harmony with its situation. Howard's quiet pictures of Jarman, of driftwood and detail, had changed everything for me about how to see space.

Jarman captures him in the book when he writes: 'Howard Sooley is a giraffe, a giraffe that has stared a long time at a photo of Virginia Woolf; he possesses the calm and sweetness of that miraculous beast.' From out of this calm – and companionship – together we would conjure our first miraculous plot and go on to make more.

1960. Christopher is obsessed with forming clubs. We have homemade badges, drawn and coloured on card, attached with safety pins. Mum is concerned about the holes in our shirts and jumpers. Our badges are usually round, sometimes shaped like shields. There are arcane rules. He is always the leader. I am the only other member. We are always a secret society because other boys are immune. We never ask girls. We make dens as meeting places. I swear loyalty to the club and Christopher. I am soon replaced by cricket.

SATURDAY JULY 11, 6AM. Under siege. The midges that hang around the pond and plot in the summer evening and early morning are attacking me. I am intent on clearing space for new growth, letting in light and air. It is already monsoony humid, threatening rain. I don't much notice the midges at first, batting them away absentmindedly, irritated by the odd bite as they penetrate gaps on my shirt sleeves, the pale flash of flesh as I bend. I clear the last of the broad beans, battered by slugs. I pull invading calendula, picking through it for cut flowers for the kitchen table, leaving the vivid orange bloom I haven't the heart to take. I thin through new-sown salad for lunch. There is much still to do when my face and arms begin to itch uncontrollably, like a child with chicken pox. While I have been working, the bugs have been feasting. I urgently need something to stop the swelling now pressing on one eye, and the raging scratching. I retire from the skirmish, stopping to grab leaves, beans and flowers, and flee.

Later, hopped on antihistamine, smothered in cortisone cream and disfigured with a leer, I return. Howard joins me. We need to sow. The twin pea beds at the bottom of both plots are failing, so we will supplement them with low-growing bush beans. It may be our last chance to sow them this year. We pull the flowering coriander and hang it on a wigwam to dry. I brought the original packet back from Brazil. It is intensely spicy – a local strain, I think. We save the seed for later. I clear another bed for wintering chicories. At the last minute I rip out the top bed too and re-sow with a black bean from Brown Envelope. The crinkled peas should have been picked while we were away. We eat a few from the pod and divide the rest. As the light dips and Howard gets bitten, we finish. In the three hours we have been here we have hardly spoken. The few words exchanged are about the benefits or not of getting a wheelbarrow and which beans are for where. Conversation picks up on the walk home down the hill.

1961. Almost as soon as Christopher and I are reunited we begin to grow apart. Nurture acing nature, if not just yet. He holds on fast to his history and name (though why this decision is his I don't understand; it should never have been). I pack myself away in search of something safer, smarter, more versatile. Like a Christmas cowboy suit, like dressing up. My identity is broken, soon it will be time to try on Peter Drabble; from underclass to middle class, like the jacket in the first photograph that didn't yet fit. I often imagine now how my brother's life would have played out if Lilian and Dudley had called him Christopher Drabble. In my head he is smiling, happily married, with many dogs and kids, maybe managing an arable farm in Canada. His life would have had more choices.

Herons Reach is on the Stakes Road across the mud flats, half a mile from school if the tide is out, a mile if it is in. I love messing on the river on my own, while Christopher loves the village. He is bigger now, brilliant at head-butting me, but I can feel his fragility. Sense the uncertainty. See it when no one else is interested. He will come to rely on his fists. I will rely on my wits.

The change will come between us often. Rural Devon in the Sixties is still remote. A place where brothers have the same names, the same features, the same interests. We are different, and difference is difficult.

Other boys too are to be discouraged, at least at home. In our first year there is a birthday party but this is to be the last. Lilian doesn't like boys or parties in her house – too noisy, too messy, too muddy, too hard-edged. Softness for me is to be found in other kids' homes, a warmer welcome with a tender touch. Boys don't much come around again, not even for Christopher and he collects friends like I collect stamps. He starts spending his days at the farm next door, walking the fields, helping call in the cows, bringing home milk and mud. The farmer is handsome, young, in his twenties, a bachelor, though this thought has only struck me now. I prefer to stick closer to home, closer to Lilian and Dudley, watching as she pares the runner beans he grows into neat piles of wafer-thin green. Food is always simple, almost always freshly grown. For Dudley, as for Mary's husband Don, runner beans signal English summer.

SUMMER 2007. Ruth's allotment is slowly taking shape. Howard and I have spent weeks up to our knees, thighs sometimes, trenching out bricks and glass, wire and wood, tree stumps and concrete posts, while Don looks approvingly on. Mary leaves us small bags of salad as encouragement. One day, the allotment association steps in. They hire a skip and I arrive mid-morning to find a fireman's chain of wheelbarrows to run the rubble up. It seems everyone is here to help.

Sarah turns up from the advertising department of the *Guardian* where I work. Who knew wellingtons came with high heels? She helps me spread five tonnes of topsoil we've brought in to slow the slope. She learns to kill slugs and snails. She drives 300 miles with me to pick up a lorry load of cow manure. 'Horses' energy is too fast for vegetables but fine for flowers, you need cow', was the opaque advice from Jane Scotter. The manure is a gift from a farmer who had answered a plea put out into the biodynamic community. It's harder than you think to find organic cow muck in London. We drive back delicately in our hired, loaded-down flat-back truck (we have been a bit vague about what we want it for, failing to mention manure). We are barely making it up the hills, laughing, almost choking, in a heavy fug of farmyard.

The slope is tamed now, the soil is fed. We are ready to grow.

July

The Danish agricultural museum has sent us 'lost' seed, including Tagetes Ildkonge (for Christopher), the deepest-red, most velvety marigolds we have ever seen. Sarah and I plant a large bed of perpetual spinach. We have a wigwam of fragrant sweet peas and another of purple-podded Trail of Tears. The tagetes grow to a thick hedge. We have herbs, fennel, flowers, beetroot, carrots, kale, mustards, green manure. I set a national competition for school gardening clubs to design a scarecrow and have the magazine fashion team build and dress the winner. Soon a six-foot scarlet pirate, complete with eye-patch, hat and silvery sword, guards against the resident pigeons. They ignore him. We plant an apple tree, a plum tree, gooseberry and currant bushes – just like Dad. Everything we sow grows lush like rainforest, as though its energy had been imprisoned and is now unleashed. The allotment is happy and so are we, but I can't bear to thin and throw the weakest tomatoes – maybe I identify with their need, preferring to give them more light and food and love. Soon we have 20 plants, tall and fruiting in the sunniest spot at the top of the plot. We don't know blight is endemic on the site and that nurturing rain also spreads disease. Their leaves start to brown and buckle. The tomatoes too. Seedlings I have nursed from birth are sickening and dying, and there is nothing I can do. Throughout the site, tomato plants are failing. The weakest die first, of course, their fruits blistered, their stems and leaves discoloured. Seasoned allotment holders strip the leaves and spray them, like a field hospital for failing plants. Still they fail. Like plague before penicillin. In the end we pull them all and cart their corpses to the green bin by the gate. No compost renewal now.

PLOT 29

A gardening lesson in love and loss. But one I am reluctant to learn.

SUMMER 1973. My first garden in London is in Elgin Avenue, a street of squats near Notting Hill Gate. I am 19, working for a garden centre in Kensington, selling window-box flowers to posh west London ladies. Here, it seems, everyone buys their gardens ready made, no time to wait. This is gardening as competitive sport. I have become skilled at persuading neighbours to upgrade over each other. If one has bought red geraniums and a three-foot window box in terracotta, I'll sell next door a three-and-a-half-foot in stone and with better, bigger flowers. No one grows from seed. There is a lot of waste. This is new to me. I start carting home pots of dried-out azalea rescued from the bins. Soon I have buckets of rehydrating bushes inside and outside the flat, front and back. I nurture my waifs back to life. As the garden fills up, I start planting out the rest. The speed freaks don't much mind as long as they don't have to water. I spread down the street as fast as the dealers spread up. We have azaleas, geraniums, pelargoniums, magnolia, a bay tree slightly bent out of shape. There should be an award for the best-dressed street of squats.

JULY 17. The temperature has been in the high twenties for the past three days and I have promised Mary I'll water. She is taking a break in Cornwall and I want the plot to look well in time for her return. Howard and I head up before breakfast. I love the light at this time, fruit trees and bushes backlit by the low early sun. Our neighbour Jeffrey is an American banker with a passion for English cottage gardens. His fennel and hollyhocks are two metres tall. Bees stream from the next-door hives like *Star Wars* fighter squadrons. A fledgling robin, head cocked, watches us. Red amaranth and bull's blood chard stand in contrast to the other, younger lime-green leaves. All is right in allotment world. Howard waters while I take more calendula, mildew at its base a warning signal of autumn. Time for the borders to breathe, time for beans. Of course we have too many (the seed finally pulled though). Feeler vines outstretch like a drowning man's hand. Howard is buttoned up against bugs but still they get through. The anxious scratching starts.

SEPTEMBER 1959. The village school test for TB has alarmed Mum and Dad and me. My left arm is very swollen, with red streaks running down. And the doctor thinks I am 'rickety'. Christopher is OK, which only means more mystery. Where was I? Where was he? The first clue we maybe hadn't always been together. But why our amnesia?

Rickets. A Dickensian world away from the family life the Drabbles have been building. No vitamin D and now I am touched by TB. Capital letters writ large of lack of care. Where was family, where was safety, where was my other mum? It had been beaten into us at the home, this cross we carry. We are either unlovable or the cursed brood of an unloving mother. Either way, we need to be quarantined from the herd. Mums are meant to be like

Mary, a loving Christian icon clutching her baby to her breast.

For the next 10 years I have an annual X-ray, looking for lesions. My sunken chest pressed against cold metal, standing on tiptoe on a box, straining chin on top. Would my past incubate? Would it return to disturb me? I have a large spoonful of cod liver oil every morning now, shuddering as it sluices down. I also have a memory of being given raw liver, but this may be elaboration or invention, a common failing for kids like me.

I invented my father once. There was a man who regularly used to watch as we played on the roundabout in the park at the back of the Plymouth home. I told everyone he was my dad. (I didn't say he was Christopher's; maybe my brother wasn't there. My memories are sketchy and episodic, pixelated like worn VHS tape. No one to top them up.) The mystery man was watching over me, waiting, I told the other kids. He would be coming soon to take me away when he had found a place for us to stay. I didn't understand when he didn't come.

JULY 19, SATURDAY. It's sweltering after two nights of thunderstorms, with temperatures hitting 32°C. There's no more need to water, at least for now. I hit the plot in the late afternoon to check on progress. I have been sowing Mary's 'pumpkin plot' with squash and courgette seed and I'm happy to see new plants popping through. I fork up a few potatoes, blushing Red Duke of York. As a child, I loved to dig the potatoes for weekend lunch, lifting them in the hour before eating. They were always King Edward's, boiled with apple mint when new, diligently scraped and served with salty butter. We grew peas, runner beans, strawberries (Dudley's favourite) but it was from potatoes I learned the joy of growing food for the table, taking as much as you need for the meal and no more.

JULY 20. Back on the first bus, early Sunday morning. The success of the squash seed has inspired me to weed the pit and move Mary's bags of manure. It's not yet 7am and I am smeared with insect repellent and horse shit that has liquified in the heat. It is steamy, mucky work as I stack the sacks. I hoe through the bed, move a stray calendula and sow courgette seed. I am prone to over-sow, almost as though my faith in things is thin and I still don't quite believe in miracles. (I do. I think I almost am one.) I weed through Mary's beetroot, beans and chard and cull the choking strawberry runners. The first beans are ready on the first wigwam: blue Blauhilde and Trail of Tears. I pick a handful to add to the potatoes. We will have them steamed and served with butter, just like Mum and Dad. My boots and trousers are smeared with manure. My shirt is soaked with sweat. My hair is sticking to my head. I am happy. A smart matron with two blazered schoolgirls pulls them closer to her as I pass. I am not dressed for Sunday society or even for the bus. Hampstead should have a tradesmen's entrance.

JULY 22. Each garden in my life has its own identity, fulfils a different function, but the oldest and perhaps purest is the roof terrace at home. It was tiled with asbestos and packed with junk and dead bicycles when we moved in. I went a little mad at first, turning it into a country-cottage garden above an urban street. It was a riot of colour and contrast. The walls were trestled, none left bare. Roses rambled and added scent. Jasmine too. Early- and late-flowering clematis came next. We covered the floor in marble pebbles, brought in a weathered teak table and chairs. We eat dinner there on a summer evening, drink tea in our coats with the newspapers in winter. The roof terrace keeps me connected to the countryside. It's an oasis of calm in Kentish Town. Pots are planted for colour, always brighter in summer.

Its identity has changed, matured with us. First to go were the trestles, the climbing plants and the once-white stones. Flowers became more individual, picked for personality, but there are always dahlias. Dudley thought them 'common' but I love them for their myriad shapes and strong colours as they ease the shift into autumn. There is a *Magnolia stellata* because its flowers signal early spring but mostly the roof terrace is a gateway to our piece of sky, a place to potter outside.

1959. We have our own bedroom, our own bed. But the truest sign of home is our dressing gowns. To be worn watching TV or after a Sunday-night bath, shiny for the new school week, downstairs for a goodnight peck, ours are brown wool, plain with a piped edge. My cord is blue and white, Chris's is red and white like a barber's pole, the colours of Manchester United, his favourite football team. Local Plymouth Argyll lose too often for his liking.

July

1960. Seven-year-old Christopher looks like Alfred E. Neuman from *Mad* magazine: gap-toothed, freckle-faced, wide cheeky grin. He is growing. The past is beginning to fade. He has slipped its grip. He is made for village life. It is more forgiving than Mum and Dad. He rediscovers his appetite. He comes in from outside (he is always outside) to wolf down fuel for the afternoon. Roaming like a puppy, seeing what he can find. He is what he says on the tin: an eager kid who deserves a break, who'll adore you if you adore him. It almost works, in the heady days before Lilian and Dudley's caustic disappointment becomes more marked. He is alert, senses it long before I do.

Christopher tells me stories at night as we lie excited in our matching beds with matching candlewick bedspreads. I am jealous of his teddy bear with its stitched black nose and articulated limbs. I have a stuffed white Scotty dog, its legs too stiff and short to hug. We wear matching Ladybird Cosijamas, fleeced inside, no strings or buttons, almost American. We can't believe our luck sometimes, like we have landed on the moon. Safety like we had dreamed of, a family like we'd hoped. The storytelling lasts about a year, not every night but nearly as often as I ask. They are mostly adventure yarns: pirates. I am big on pirates. The river calls me from outside our window, occasional small boats elevated into three-masted ships, skull and crossbones flying, bearded ear-ringed men, heavily armed, sabres between their teeth. I am an impressionable child, overexcited in the summer light. Christopher is kind. We are close.

1961. Christopher is left-handed. Neither Dudley nor the school approves. Both try to train it out of him. It is suspect in some way, 'other', an unnatural, un-Christian thing. The teacher hits his left hand with a wooden pencil case. He walks up behind him. Sometimes nothing is said. It is as though left is a link to the wild, to be suppressed. With Dudley, it is just 'different'. Fitting in is a thing with him, no standing out. We are learning to be invisible, at the expense of Chris's hand. It doesn't work, of course. Christopher is good at being hit.

1962. I like to scare myself as a child. There is a tree in the darkest part of the lane behind the house where I like to linger. It is tall, maybe malevolent, its branches and bark twisted like something from Tolkien. Christopher always hurries past (though he is braver than me with bullies). I stop and wait, savouring the moment of fear as scary branches wave in the wind. By about 10 or 11 years old, I have graduated to an abandoned badger sett I find on one of my long walks along the river. It is buried into the bank. I crawl deep inside, under the exposed roots, the heavy Devon clay. Burrow in as far as I can. I lie there daring the roof to fall, to bury me in red soil. The appeal is enhanced by the feeling I might never be found, the thought I can just disappear. After maybe half an hour of lying there I go home for lunch. By age 12, I get kicks from a piece of shaley cliff where the path had been eroded. I look down at the white water and rocks, and slide. You can't walk it, do it carefully. The only route is surrender, to guide the drop to a piece of broken path with your feet. I love to let go, see if I can cross to the other side, stand where no one else would dare. I never do it with anyone else. Secrecy is the thing. I grow out of it when I become interested in girls.

1963. Lilian's mother has come to live (or more accurately, die) with us. Christopher has to give up his bedroom and move back in with me. It's not going well. He is not happy and when he is not happy we fight and I lose. At least he is outdoors all day, while I am obliged to stay in and read to her. She sends me to the village to buy her bottled stout. Mum and Dad are teetotal, the only booze the Christmas cherry liqueur and Harvey's Bristol Cream on the sideboard for guests who never come.

Mum and Dad don't read, except Dudley's local *Western Morning News*. There is only a scant handful of ancient books in the house. The old grandma is a bit bad-tempered and I don't like the smell of her or her beer, but I am fascinated by her age, her drab clothes, her thin, lined mouth and the thought that she is near to death. So we sit in the curtain-drawn gloom in the summer afternoon and I read her *Heidi*. She is 84, from deep in the nineteenth century, like my Victorian stamps and coins, too far away for a small boy to comprehend. She dies one night while we are asleep. We don't get to see her or go to her funeral, though we are allowed to join the tea with Lilian's good tableware. Christopher is soon moved back to his room.

1964. Mum cuts our hair with clippers: old school, hand action, blunt. She is always snagging our necks. She is worse at cutting a fringe. I think she is nervous. So are we. Christopher screams like he is being butchered. He checks for blood. He hates sitting still. I think we are all relieved when crew cuts come in and we can go to the barber in Kingsbridge. They let me take a sneak through *Parade* and pore over its pictures of topless girls. They also have *Health and Efficiency* – smaller, less sexy pages of naked ping pong in a naturist magazine. I leave feeling almost a teenager, splashed with spritz.

JULY 23. Of course I am now concerned about the baby squash and courgettes in the heatwave. The weather has been baking for days, so I am back on the first bus with today's bleary-eyed postal workers. It's bright, the start of a maybe 30-degree day, but there's cool in the early-morning air, the first spectral tendril of autumn. The plot will need water and I can be back home before breakfast. Bill is there when I arrive, communing with his allotment, waiting for the day. We talk a little about the benefits of growing seed at home. It gives them a head start, he says. A heavy wave of sweet pea hits me as I pass the corner by the plot. A pigeon is feasting on the elder at the end of the plot, flapping its wings anxiously to maintain its greedy balance. The berries are turning now. Autumn won't be long. Mary's runner bean wigwam is flecked with flower and the bush beans are breaking through. I am more worried about the borders. Bindweed is creeping its way into the strawberry bed and the lovage is being tethered to the ground like Gulliver, sporting parasitic blooms. I grab a handful of beans. I have been bitten again and am starting to scratch. I soak the pumpkin bed, grinning at the new growth. Watering may be the best feeling in gardening. By 7am I am back on the bus, refreshed. I need breakfast and a bath.

SUMMER 1964. I have an appointment to be beaten. It is my choice. Dudley had been renting the field to the farmer for his cows to pasture but some escaped. It is our fault. Christopher and I have made a den in the hedge, a hideout for outlaw brothers after robbing a stagecoach or train. But the cows broke through and one became trapped in the river mud. I remember it lowing down the valley as the tractor tries to pull it out. It is freed eventually, it doesn't drown, but the farmer's nearly lost a beast and Dad is incandescent. He decides we can choose our punishment: to be caned or to miss TV for a week. No great loss, I think. We have BBC until 7pm, *Dixon of Dock Green* on Saturdays, maybe *Doctor Who*. The only person who can pick up ITV is the local coroner, who is given dispensation for a giant mast in the garden for his aerial, maybe because he spends his days with the dead.

Christopher goes for the TV option. I choose the beating. Just before bed I head downstairs in my dressing gown. I am scared but I want the anger over. Christopher waits, the thought of (another) beating unbearable. Mum and Dad are sitting in the living room by the anthracite fire. He has a garden cane beside him, a few cream crackers and cheese, a blue mug of Ovaltine. It is almost as though he is worried he will need a snack to replenish his strength. I am bent over his knee, my dressing gown has been removed. I think I am crying. I am hit once, maybe twice, but he doesn't have the heart. After half an hour of Z-*Cars*, I return upstairs, triumphant but tear-stained. Christopher is angry I've almost escaped. I am furious the next day when his sentence is rescinded. There is no justice.

JULY 27. I had to leave the allotment yesterday; it was too hot to garden. I had contented myself with moving a few sunflowers and courgettes. I haven't grown sunflowers for a while; the last were self-seeded. They grew like Jack and the Beanstalk, creating a shadowy canopy three metres tall. But I discovered seed in the bottom of my bag and I couldn't control myself. I pick through radishes. They are big, round and red like kids' lollipops but eat like crisp, mustardy apples. I cut lettuce for lunch and chard for weekday dinners, and gather a few multi-coloured handfuls of beans. It is too hot to work: days of mad dogs and Englishmen.

First thing Sunday morning, I am back. It's cooler now so I lift the last of the calendula, tying a favoured yellow flower to the wigwam to save for seed. I weed through vegetable beds and train sweet peas. Mostly, though, this morning is about watering. I might not get back now for a couple of days so I soak everything in. The allotment site feels a bit abandoned. I miss seeing Mary.

1964. Being in the church choir is unavoidable for a village boy in Aveton Gifford. Only posh and 'problem families' are exempt. It is an infallible way to tell. Every week we pull cassock and surplice over our Sunday best and add our unbroken voices to the service. I faint once in the summer when the air is heavy, and come around to the sound of my feet drumming on the raised wooden floor. Wednesday evening is choir practice. There is sometimes a wedding on Saturday. Dudley never goes to church. Lilian goes twice a year: Easter and Mothering Sunday, when the church distributes the bunches of primroses we have gathered in the week. My favourite service is harvest festival. Hymns about ploughing fields, altar bread shaped like a sheath of corn, a table of fruit, vegetables, flowers and a few random tins of soup.

I don't much like the vicar and he doesn't like me. I don't do sports, play cricket or football in the vicarage grounds like other boys, although Christopher excels at both. I prefer my own company, which the vicar doesn't trust. One Wednesday evening, waiting for choir practice to start, I decide to stay outside in the sun. Christopher's plan to blackmail me is undone a couple of days later by a knock on the door. The vicar and the village policeman (it seems bunking off village choir is close to a crime in the Sixties) stand there. Dad doesn't invite them in. They think he should know, the vicar says. Perhaps bad blood will out. A priest and cop have come to our house. I have brought disgrace. I return to church and the choir, lesson learned. Back to singing solo, back to Advent weekend afternoons touring old people's homes in brown-face and a beard and crown, a king in a Christmas carol. The vicar is probably right, I think. A rebellion has begun.

Muhammad Ali is our first hero, still called Cassius Clay when we listen to his fights on the radio (the wireless, as Dad always calls it). Christopher at first prefers Sonny Liston, impressed by his brutal efficiency. Dudley disapproves of them both but despises Clay's cockiness. I love his swagger. Christopher and I don't share other heroes, except Eusébio in the football World Cup in 1966. Christopher is for mop-top Paul and Ringo, I am for George and John. We don't often like the same music or people but Ali is a unifying force. Christopher admires him for his boxing; I love him outside the ring.

1965. Dudley is prone to strange schemes and fancies. The Christmas trees, the poor chinchillas he keeps caged in a shed. The barn is converted for battery chickens, stacked high like Tesco. There are two sets of lights, one white, one red. The sight of blood from a crushed or cut bird sends the house into a frenzy but switching the light turns the red blood brown and the birds soon settle. I am never quite happy in the barn, picking eggs, spotting corpses. The mis-sexed young cockerels are the first to go. Don't call so loud and proud, I want to warn when they show off their crow. My dad will hunt you down.

One day, two white goats appear. Dad's been reading *Farmers Weekly*. We drive them miles to be mated, the first step to producing milk. I have never come across anything that stinks like a stud billy goat and wonder why Lilian and I are watching while they have sex. Must be a farmer thing, I think. I became fond, though, of the nannies in the field behind the house, fascinated as their bellies balloon. I think their babies will be like having lambs (Christopher is forever coming home with stories of rejected young sheep being kept in an Aga drawer). The big day comes. I rush home from school. There are no cute baby kids gambolling in the paddock or nuzzling their mother's milk. I am confused. They were male so I clubbed them, Dudley tells me matter of fact. When I ask where their graves are, he points to the cesspit. I think I hate him a little that day.

The main trouble with the goats is no one likes their milk. We are having it in tea, on cereal, on our porridge. We are spared from drinking it straight. Dad is the first to switch. I am soon back to picking up his milk from the farm. We kids have to stick with goat for a while: it is good for growing boys, he's read. But one day they have disappeared, as though they never happened. I wonder why we don't get to say goodbye. I don't go near goat's cheese for 20 years.

There is a photograph of me in my final year of primary school. I am sitting up straight, blond hair neatly combed, looking into the camera, superior smile on my face. Pure Midwich Cuckoo, pure Peter Drabble. The rescue operation appears complete. Like our river cottage, I have been rebuilt into something smarter. Gone for now the questioning eyes, to be replaced with over-weening confidence. I am head boy at my small Church of England school, garlanded in gushing valentines and the 11-plus. Grammar school is next. There is also, though, an uneasiness about my last year there. A girl from the estate is humiliated in class. She renders the summer sky yellow, the wheat field blue. I like the paint-ing's boldness, its originality, but the teacher humiliates her, toys with her like a cat showing kittens how to torture mice. We are being taught about more than English and maths. This is a lesson in class, about who her parents are.

Christopher is becoming crueller. The hunted grows to be the hunter; the abuser rather than the abused. It is simple, the psychology. The Drabbles have withdrawn their favour. His hurt has to be displaced. He turns to shooting random birds and rabbits; breaking wings, breaking legs. He sends in dogs. He turns on Mum and Dad, snarls his anger. He turns on me. I am blinded by other loyalties, too young and stupid to see. He grows to like a fight, my brother; is more of a force at school (I have sometimes cause to be grateful). Ironically, by the time he is a boxer in the army, Dudley brings him back into the family fold. It is my turn to be exiled.

Christopher is already at secondary school in Kingsbridge, the local market town, learning to curse, spray power words around like cunt and fuck and twat. He is a Jenkins, running with a tougher town crowd, I am a Drabble, still tied to my village primary. By the time I get to Kingsbridge, the grammar and secondary schools have merged, the new comprehensive classes streamed. I am in 1.1, year one, top tier, Christopher in 2.5. Our drift apart is official, as if we are not brothers any more. What we had is almost invisible.

It isn't until secondary school that I realise how old my mum and dad are. It is a year of Bob Dylan, The Beatles, the Rolling Stones and Sandie Shaw. BBC newsreaders sport longer hair, longer collars, wider and brighter ties. Dad watches The Supremes on TV and says unfortunate things. Other kids have posters in their bedroom, their fathers will grow their hair. Lilian and

Dudley are 20 to 30 years older than the parents of other kids in my class, their lives forever defined by the war. Even their names speak of another century.

Each year of the mid Sixties adds a half-decade to the differences between us. The questions they have raised me to ask become more difficult. What about apartheid and Vietnam, I demand, though their politics never waver. Clothing becomes an issue. We aren't allowed jeans. I pine for a pair of Levi's. I take a paper round and start buying records, though we only have a radio for Dudley's classical concerts. The person I want to be is being redefined, away from Mum and Dad's plan. I must be a source of worry to them.

From five to 13, I have loved my village life, our dog, our donkey, but now I long for a life less defined by who my mother and father are. Lilian despairs, the threats to 'send us back' increase, her love less unconditional by the day. Dudley becomes more angry while I become more defiant. Christopher sulks and stays away ever longer.

It isn't yet hopeless. I am doing well at school, and Christopher is promoted a class each year: 2.5 became 3.4, 4.3: an A-level stream, but we don't know our childhood is over, a chill teenage winter is coming. A care crisis plan is about to be put into action. We will never be the same. I have stupidly forgotten the lesson about always earning conditional love.

AUGUST

AUGUST 3. Plot 29. Two days of hoeing, digging, raking – clearing weeds from Mary's beds. Her broad beans have gone over, pods fat and ripe, hanging heavy, waiting for her. The onion bed is also overgrown. Greedy calendula has taken over, with sycamore seedlings in support. Bindweed by the wheelbarrow-load has been creeping in, smothering other plants. Mary's cold frame is nurturing weed. Attack is the best defence.

Bindweed to the waste bin, calendula to the compost, seedy perpetual spinach too. I clear the frame and lay out a sack for onions and shallots. It is sweaty work in sultry weather but we need clean beds to sow. September is only four weeks away, the sun is starting to dip, sap is beginning to slow.

By teatime Sunday, I am sitting, hands a bit torn, shirt a bit sticky, when I hear my name behind me. Mary's standing there, a little tired. I show off the beds like a proud schoolboy handing in his homework. She smiles. We talk about her crop rotation. She has a plan at home she says she will send me. We admire the runner beans and the sweet peas I have just finished tying (the sweetest-smelling job). The pumpkin bed is thriving. Her courgettes are flowering and the rest not far behind. She gathers herbs and rocket and beans. I press her to take some of our chard and red-hearted lettuce. Howard and his family are on holiday and I am daunted by how lush everything is. Mary hands me seed to sow. I'll be back in a couple of days.

1968. It is decided I should go to boarding school. Plymouth children's department will pay and there will be a scholarship. I am mostly messing about at Kingsbridge but coming top or near it in exams. My French master hates me for it. My writing is sloppy, a source of shame to Dad, whose copperplate is immaculate. The teacher makes me rewrite my French exercise book overnight. It starts neatly until I see it is too slow. He slippers me the next day. Punishment is measured in strikes of three or six, with the teacher's choice of weapon (he favours a gym shoe) on your non-writing hand. The notebook is worth six, the small man almost jumping as he hits. After he's finished, I smirk my contempt. He has me hold out my right hand for another six. I walk back to my seat in angry tears, girls are looking up at me, sad.

It isn't just schooling. Mum and Dad are worried about sex, about me spending time with girls in their bedrooms listening to Jimi Hendrix. Dad loathes Hendrix, his black sexuality. The girls' allure is almost as much in the soft colours and fabrics of their pop-postered rooms (mine is austere, almost military) as the thought I can slip a hand in underwear. Mum particularly seems obsessed by the idea of sex. Maybe it is the fear of my feral other mother. Christopher, meanwhile, contents himself with football and fighting, hanging out at the village pub.

Changes are coming, decisions have been made. The threats to send us back to Plymouth are more relentless. It is over. We are out. Boarding school and the army are presented as Mum and Dad's only options for our future. I like the idea at first. It sounds like an adventure. I am good at new people and places. I have practice.

Christopher pleads to stay on at school for agricultural college, his grades have improved every year. He loves our neighbour's farm and farming, is dug in deep in the village. He belongs here like no one else. I am too smart-mouthed, too strange, Lilian and Dudley too stand-offish. But Dad is insistent. Christopher is packed off early to the army. He will never forget or forgive them and I am not sure I do. In the summer of '68, as the rest of the world seems set to change, our family fractures. It is sudden, savage, the shift.

AUGUST 5, 7.30AM. An early weekday visit to the allotment. I keep a shirt in the shed for watering or weeding, in case I have a meeting first thing and don't want to be wearing mud. I am here to sow, easier in the morning air. I cut sticks and string, give the bed another hoe. There will be short rows, some with Mary's seed and a couple of cavolo nero, lettuce, red mustard and rocket. A blackbird lays the soundtrack and a robin keeps me company. A few feet away, pigeons hang in the skeleton tree like vultures waiting for something to die. Within an hour or so the sowing is done. I water it in. The forecast is for rain but I can't resist soaking the rest of the plot. The beans and squash are greedy and it relaxes me before the bus to work (no time to walk now). Mary will have her autumn leaves. I wander around, reluctant to leave. The corn looks as if it is ready to eat, the cobs are fat, but they will have to wait till Howard is back. A young black cat, no collar, passes by nervously.

1968. Battisborough House is set back from a cliff not far from Plymouth. It is a Kurt Hahn school, the Outward Bound man, whose most famous school is Gordonstoun, where Prince Charles has just been head boy. Its reputation is based on character-building. No one goes to Battisborough for its academic excellence, though it is there in its small class size and dedicated teachers. It is founded on a Germanic ideal crossed with an English public-school ethos. There is emphasis on activities. We wear two uniforms: navy blue for the morning and grey for after tea. No ties or blazers but open-neck shirts and sweaters and corduroy shorts (tough if, like me, you think shorts are for summer or primary school), long flannels for church. There are no girls, except a couple of teachers' daughters who live on the grounds. I wonder if they are ever as longed for again. I date one, the same age as me. We kiss. I rub her skirt and shirt. There is to be no beating, an ethos from the headmaster, David Byatt, who leads by example. I am to test this resolve. The boys who are good at boarding school are the ones unbroken by starting there aged seven (there are, of course, casualties), followed by the boys who start at 11. The odds are against boys who arrive aged 14 because they cannot live at home and still call themselves part of a family.

I love my first year here, though it is at Battisborough I discover my Devon accent, a shock when the Sony machine replays my village burr, less of a shock when other boys mimic it. There is a maximum intake of 60 pupils, though it is down to 36, little more than a class at Kingsbridge. I absorb it all like tissue, the English classes of maybe eight, with a teacher who is interested. 'You like Herman Hesse, try Günter Grass.' Wives also teach. I am impressionable, eager, almost desperate to learn. It looks as if it will work. I jump a year in English, Maths and French (no psychopathic slippering here, a less messy exercise book). Every afternoon there are sports, though I am less keen on this. I hate rugby in winter. There are other activities – tennis at the courts of the local land-owner's house or gardening. I tend plants and trees and hide behind rhododendrons to smoke Player's No 6, the schoolkids' cigarette of choice. But the afternoons I like best involve cross-country running, unleashed like a lurcher over cliffs, across beaches and along my beloved south Devon estuaries, very nearly free. Battisborough is also where I learn more subtle social lessons, that class and cars matter. Frugality can be suspect. At the end of term a procession of vehicles comes to pick us up – wide Mercedes, fat American convertibles, and the air-cooled splutter of Dudley's little Fiat 500, not yet the cult car it will become. But I am happy, I know I can adapt. I have done it before.

AUGUST 8. Glorious. Crimson sky. Every day, autumn tightens its grip. Timing is important, crops for winter have to be established before the light and warmth fade too far and energy retreats. Autumn and winter salad mixes must go in, late radishes and hardy herbs. Plans, such as they are, start to be formulated in my head. There is a thought of green manure this year: clover, physalis, vetch. The question is how much of the plot should be covered and what Mary wants. There will be digging to do, a war on weed.

1968. Dad isn't one for swearing, an occasional bloody if Mum isn't around. So when Christopher tells me what bugger and prat mean it sounds implausible. The only time with Dad is once in the car when he crashes the gears. We're alone. I am 14. Old enough to hear him say fuck.

All change. We cannot find your mother but we have found your sister Lesley and your father, the care worker tells me (this use of 'care' in 'children in care' a Goebbels-like lie). Things are drifting dangerously at home, Christopher is unhappy in the army. I am away at boarding school. Dad has sold Herons Reach to Lilian's nephew, who wants a bolt hole from Kuwait. Gone the river, gone the field, broken the sense of security. Dudley is clearing the decks.

I am wanting to know more about Alan Jenkins. Mum and Dad are probably resentful, though they have never said so. It is as though it is a matter of poor manners and ingratitude, not identity. Asking is discouraged throughout the system. It is wrong, the 'right to know'. I am searching for an escape plan. If one door closes, can another open? But if Lilian and Dudley don't want us, why would anyone?

A photo strip arrives at school of a skinhead girl grinning into the camera. I pore over it. Can I see a likeness? It will be a first for me (Christopher and I are never alike in looks or temperament, though tightly bound together like corn). Most families share the same eyes, smile, same mouth. They swim in a sea of recognition, reassured of where they belong. I think I have always been longing for a face that could be connected to me.

My sister and I exchange excited messages. Lesley writes of her life in Basildon, a new town in Essex, with her – 'our' – dad. I show off from my posh Devon school.

I cannot discuss it at home, the wheels are coming off. But I pine for Lesley's letters, like adolescent love.

I have long wanted a sister, someone soft. Perhaps finding a dad is less important because Dudley has filled that space. A mum, though, is different, a primeval pull. It isn't anyone's fault, just how it is. Maybe, as we get older and more male, Lilian still mourns the baby girl she never had.

I worry why she isn't more affectionate. Kisses, quick cuddles are for when I am sick. I had divined early on that it was because she was too thin, her breasts couldn't carry enough chemicals for love. Other boys' mums are more curved, more tactile, invite you in, feed you, sit on the same sofa as their sons. I am envious of friends who are held. It has been a long time. I am in need of mothering.

There isn't, though, a mother to be found, the care worker says. For now, a sister and a father will do. Letters are exchanged from our twin alien worlds. Lesley's handwriting is neat and loopy, sometimes comes in green ink.

For the first time, the end of the summer term means a train on my own to London and not a short Devon drive. I am at Paddington Station and my name is called over the Tannoy. Will I come to the station manager's office. I am sick, a little scared. We would have had counselling for it now, this seismic shift in who we are. The tidal pull of blood and belonging.

Suddenly we are in the same room, family parted 10 years before. Lesley with her Prince of Wales pattern skirt and long, green nails, her Essex accent and smile. With my dad, Ray, it is different, something is wrong, though not from his side. He isn't the man I expected to see, the one I've been waiting for. I rationalise it later: how could anyone live up to the hope, the longing I have buried? I had Hollywooded the moment: the glamorous sailor back from the sea, the white fence with Mum and me waiting. Ray is taking me home, what more could I want?

Basildon is impossible. A New Town, an east London overspill, surrounded by a ring of factories: Ford, Ski yoghurt, Carreras cigarettes. Lesley, my sister, is called after Dad, Leslie Ray. I am a village kid from Devon, who has nearly been to London once on a long day trip to Heathrow Airport with Sunday school (people used to do that, a glimpse of the future and the rest of the planet through pilots and 'aeroplanes'). Otherwise my world is limited to a twice-yearly trip to Plymouth, once in summer to buy shoes and again before Christmas to buy the Norwegian sweater (mine in blue, Christopher's in red) that is always our present. We have lunch in the department-store restaurant, maybe a film if there is something suitable.

Basildon is bewildering. Identical estates laid on an identical grid, but I stay for the summer holidays, hanging around the record store to listen to music in booths or at the swimming pool by Ray and Lesley's flat, if I don't get lost (I am always lost). I am fascinated by Lesley, the way she speaks, the way she's dressed, her taste in skinhead music, her feather-cut friends, the soap operas she watches. My relationship with Ray is more complicated. He won't talk about my mother, show me photos, even tell me her name. He refuses to speak about his life with her or his wedding. 'You must never ask me, it is better you never know!' It feels odd to hit a wall so soon.

Ray is a cook but also a Pentecostal evangelist to be seen proclaiming the name of the Lord in Basildon town centre every Saturday. It is like living in a soap series I have never watched but Lesley does, *Crossroads* or *Coronation Street*. The connection to the past I have pined for still feels far away. I finally have sex, though, with a girl from the swimming pool on a piece of waste ground outside town. She is older, has more body hair, but it is a bit boring. Another disappointment, another longing unresolved.

1987. I am in need of a birth certificate for a new passport but it seems I don't exist. Alan Jenkins born on my birthday isn't to be found. I am confused, so ask at the enquiries desk. Search the adoption register, the man says, if you are not there, your birthdate is wrong. Most of my life I have carried the understanding of caste, that although they had changed my name, had played our parents, the Drabbles didn't adopt us. I was never sure why we hadn't made the grade. I was proud to bear the mark of foster child but adoption is another level of belonging, gossamer close to never having to worry about being sent back, no longer on sufferance. A family of your own. A place to stay.

I search the adoption register. And immediately there it is in black and white. All this time, my history mouldering, smouldering, in this London room. Alan Jenkins's certificate. Adopted by Leslie Ray Jenkins, it says, at 12 months old. I am lost. I had wanted a passport, a long-haul holiday, not the fabric of who I am to lie threadbare in my lunch break.

The missing feeling at 14 when we'd first met at Paddington Station wasn't a fantasy; something really wasn't right with Ray. But why adoption, not an affida-vit? He must have married my mother. I switch certifi-cates, search marriage registers, turning pages for the quarters before my adoption date. Of course she is here: Lesley Raymond Jenkins marries Sheila Irene Beale. Cafe waitress. My mother. Her name at last, like a faded photo. Radioactive information. Identity uranium.

The next step is logical but I don't know if I am ready. Should I come back with someone?

Back to the birth register. And here is Allan Peter Beale, born 15.01.1954, with the note: 'see adoption register'. Me. As a baby. A penned dash on the page for a father's name. Unknown. I knew I had been Alan Jenkins, Peter Jenkins, Peter Drabble, then back again, the coat as orig-inally cut. Back to where I had started. Or so I'd under-stood. But now there is another avatar. Baby bastard Allan with two l's. Born Beale. I order the certificates, return to the office confused, elated, angry. Maybe also relieved. The guy ropes that have grounded me are again frayed.

AUGUST 10. The tail end of Hurricane Bertha arrives from the Caribbean tomorrow. Seems we always have a mini monsoon in high summer now. Today is mostly about tidying, and cropping a basket full of beans. There are too many to eat so I will share them with family and friends. I really need Howard here with his hungry kids. The weight of the blue Blauhilde vines is wrestling a wigwam to the ground. I pile in a metal pole and tether it, like trying to tack a sailing boat against a heavy wind. The chard are like giant rhubarb. One leaf and stem may be a meal for two. I thin through the chioggia. I crop lots of lettuce. The plot is embarrassingly abundant, producing more than we can eat. I have taken to passing out parcels at work like a Red Cross mercy mission; colleagues will soon start hiding. We are mostly living on greens, beans and rice, slaked in tamari sauce and sesame oil. It makes me oddly happy and reminds me of Anglesey.

1973. I am 19 and a small group of us has escaped the city to live in a slightly hapless eco commune. Keen to grow organic vegetables on the edge of the Irish Sea, we are young, with energy and optimism. You can't say the same about Anglesey. It is the era of arson, of Welsh nationalists burning out second homes. Anglesey in the Seventies doesn't much like the English. Local people particularly don't like long hair or Asians or people who are black. We are a metropolitan mix of these, so they don't much like us, or our organic veg. There is a countryside disconnect between the surrounding seas and land and what people eat. The supermarket reigns supreme, shopping is done on price. It is the early days of genocide farming – three chickens for less than a fiver, local small suppliers closing in the onslaught of multiple rows of packaged foods. They don't always help themselves much. Our village shopkeeper switches from English to scandalised whispered Welsh when we walk in with velvet coats and smelling of sandalwood oil and exotic sex. My mixed-race girlfriend is spat on in the street. Angela is from Cardiff, Welsh-born, but I tire of facing down packs of racist young men bored at the bus station. It seems our rural idyll models itself on Mississippi, not the Druid holy island we have been naively hoping for. The dream has died. Angela is lonely and pregnant. In love with someone else. She runs away. I follow her to London like a lovesick puppy. A couple of years later, the friends who stay cut their hair, swap Afghan coats for leather jackets and become the Ruts, a punk band that has a hit with 'Babylon's Burning'. They don't mean Anglesey holiday homes.

1968. I am still unsure what sparked my early rebellion: finding my sister; Dudley selling Herons Reach and what it meant; Lilian's increasing threats to send us back; the world outside the boarding-school walls. But the puberty pupa is cracking and the moth is flexing its wet wings. It may have been Vietnam, apartheid, the Paris riots, Mao, a need to connect with the world from Prague to Peking, to Chicago. But in the end it is hair. I am sick of feeling threatened like a failed asylum seeker. It is as if a bag has been placed over my head and I am standing on a rickety chair with a rope in my hand. I am in trouble at school for writing to the Cuban and Chinese embassies. I wanted a poster of Che Guevera, a copy of Mao's little red book. In my Marvel comics they are the comic enemy, but they don't feel like mine. The music I listen to has become more introspective – Dylan, The Doors – my reading, too. The trouble starts quietly at first, with a conversation about haircuts. The Easter holidays are only a couple of weeks away and the school has the barber in. Kids are coming out of the room with military short back and sides, like Elvis in the army. A small group of us stages a haircut strike. One boy shaves his head into a Mohican as a protest. He looks very odd in shorts. Our group quickly grows to a dozen, a third of the school. It is a scene from Lindsay Anderson's *If*: a fight for influence between us and the teachers and senior boys who really run the school.

First a few words about discipline: instead of beating at Battisborough, there is a system called 'penance', based on time, according to the offence. This can be handed out by boys: up to 15 minutes at a time by middle-ranking prefects to up to an hour by the senior group or teachers. Running in school can cost you, say, 15 minutes; disputing it an hour. Your time is totted up at Friday lunch and read out over tea. Your first 15 minutes are free. Up to an hour, you get up early on Saturday morning and run in singlet and shorts. If your penance is more than an hour, you copy out the *Encyclopaedia Britannica* on Saturday evening until you have served your sentence.

Any weekend away will have to wait. Character building, they call it.

A haircut strike could never end well but it seems vital at the time – not to go home like a soldier, head shaved high, when your friends' hair curls over their collar. So we refuse. The prefects threaten. The kindly headmaster pushes a boy across the room. We are stubborn. Four of us borrow money and run away. A friend lives in Plymouth so we pitch up at his flat. There is lots of shoulder-length hair, hippie girls and the wild stink of weed. We smoke our first joints. Someone has a spare acid trip, so we cast lots. Mohican boy wins. A couple of hours or so in, the deputy head's wife arrives. They knew where we were. We haven't been discreet. She has been authorised to offer a deal. The school cannot misplace four pupils. What would they tell their parents? She says we can go to our own barber at Easter if we go back with her now. Mohican boy is in no shape for school but the rest of us agree. He will follow tomorrow. No cut. No recriminations. We return, we think, in triumph, eat late-night bacon sandwiches in the English teacher's house. By the next morning, the senior boys – shorn like sheep – have lobbied the head. Mohican boy is expelled, never to be seen again. The school, as we see it, has reneged on the deal but all the kids go home that Easter weekend with lurid stories of rebellion, dope and LSD.

I am a target from here on in, my moves monitored. The senior boys are unforgiving, the memories of their humiliating haircuts fresh. The local yokel who should have been grateful, has shown his ill-bred colours. In some ways, of course, they are right. Academically I am flying. The exam board more interesting, the teachers more engaged. I am taking 'O' levels a year early. I am on track for Oxbridge, one of the brightest kids at school (the other was Mohican boy and he is now history). There are plans to join my uncle's law firm. My middle-class metamorphosis is complete.

I see Christopher in the school holiday. It isn't easy. Our lives are growing ever further apart. After a difficult start in the army he has begun to settle. He had been put in a boxing ring at camp, where he had battered the other lad. The officers have taken an interest. It was part of a summer tournament, which he won to everyone's surprise. The kid can fight. This is something he can excel at, something the army can understand. He will soon box for his regiment, and later for the army. He has found his place, they appreciate him, he will be off for winter camp, relieved of cleaning duties.

Even when Christopher fought as a child, the other boy (often me) was simply an obstacle in his way. He was relentless when he came at you. He wouldn't, or couldn't, stop. From the early days in the children's home he had learnt how to be a boy. Now he has mastered all the manly virtues. He was always more comfortable in the company of males. We are putting on adult personalities and the matching identities no longer work. He is proud of his army uniform, polishes his shoes to a mirror shine before heading down the pub, toecaps clicking, his beret set just so. He looks a little like Dudley.

When I was 10, he gave me a masterclass in cursing. Now his language is harsher, his certainties stronger. The army has given him a new lexicon of hate. 'Queers, coons, Catholics': anything different to be feared and loathed. The Northern Ireland Troubles aren't about civil rights or equality; they are about us and them, the enemy. We can't talk about it without fear of a punch in the face, and Mum and Dad are on his side. 'We don't get their like down here,' says Dudley darkly. We will never meet at Mum and Dad's again. Our links are severed, our lives from now would barely touch.

1968. Time for girls, a teen obsession with sex. Some of the Battisborough boys coming back from London have met a gaggle of convent girls on the train. There has been kissing and fumbling, an exciting exchange of address. They are boarding near Newton Abbott, not far away. The delicious seeds of destruction are sown.

That term is about 'O' levels and letters. I am writing to my sister Lesley and to a girl at the school, twin passports into an alien world, written on pale blue paper, a Basildon bond.

It is resolved we will visit the girls' school, our notes ever more urgent. We are the same small group, now three plus one: a ginger-haired Canadian boy who will pay for booze and cabs. Our cash kept in the school office is watched closely now, so we borrow in bits. An alibi is constructed. Plans made, taxis booked, we finally rendezvous under a bridge by a lake in the convent grounds. We kiss. We drink vodka. Boarding-school boys and girls learning to be together. It is almost innocent. Our sticky-fingered reverie is broken by an anxious friend. Their beds have been found empty. The whole convent had known we were coming. A few more kisses then we flee like in a Sixties film with an anxious soundtrack.

After an uncomfortable night outside Newton Abbott, hungover from excitement and lack of sleep, we return to Battisborough. Our letters have been found at the convent. They call our school. The same bad boys named in the notes are all out of bounds. Summoned into Mr Byatt's study, we simply deny it, express our innocence. They know it is us, they've read our letters, but we may have given them, too, a chance at an alibi. No one wants the nuclear option, the fallout for both schools could be catastrophic. Our crime and punishment are too awful to contemplate.

Re-enter our flame-haired friend. The next day we are back in the study, our offence laid bare. The Canadian boy has wrestled with his guilt, we are told; the terrible truth is out. The head says he is proud of him.

Names go up on the noticeboard. We are suspended (the girls all immediately expelled). Taxis come to take us away, we say goodbye, pledge lifetime loyalty. I am never to see them again. Finally, it is just me. I anxiously wait for Dad, the put-put sound of his air-cooled engine. He doesn't come. In the end, a groovy social worker picks me up, coloured shirt, long hair, loud tie. I am too much trouble, they are too old, it is too painful, too hard for my mum and dad, he says. I must understand. They didn't sign up for problems, puberty, illicit sex. They have handed me back into the city's care. Ten years. I am on my own. My Peter Drabble dream is over. I start to shed my name on the short drive to Plymouth.

AUGUST 16. I bump into Howard and Nancy on the bus. I am on the way to the plot. They are buying Nancy her first phone. She is 11 now and only a couple of weeks away from secondary school. She would have been four when we started working on the allotments, digging holes and eating sorrel with her younger sister, Rose. She will be too adult for the allotment soon.

The plot looks overgrown, there have been weeks of sun and showers. I have been proud of its production, its high summer growth, but it is matted, like a long-haired dog that's been rolling in mud. It needs work with secateurs, a careful clearing.

I am away next weekend. Then it will be August 31, the last day of summer. Autumn is only days away, 'fall' in old English, for fall of the year and leaves. The steps to the shed are littered with conkers, signalling the start of school winter term. Jeffrey's dahlias are like dinner plates. There's a cluster of fat blackberries by the compost. The signs are everywhere. I guess I have been distracted. Mary's runner beans are running to seed. I hope she gets to eat them. I pick ours, of course, and lettuce leaves for Sunday lunch, nasturtiums for the kitchen table. As I prepare to leave, Howard and Nancy arrive, so we share berries, pod a few peas. It is good to have them back.

AUGUST 17, SUNDAY AFTERNOON. Howard is at the allotment when I arrive, ham and cheese sandwich in hand. We sit for a few minutes. It has been a month or more since we have worked together at the plot. Summer has almost gone. We never talk much about what to do on the day, each gravitating to the area where we feel we need to start. Howard begins with weeding. I want to free space to replant courgettes. It is late but I have an idea to let one or two sprawl across the path, to run free if there is enough summer energy left in the sun. I had planned to lift all the potatoes but we soon have too many to eat over the next few weeks. A rethink is necessary. I start wheelbarrowing away weed and overblown salad. Howard is in the groove, holster on his hip, secateurs in hand. Plants are pulled and thrown aside like a puppy after a bone. Everything seeding is lifted except wild rocket and amaranth, too magnificent to mess with: more than a metre tall, episcopal red leaves like cloth wrapping a sacrament. The flowering has started, shaped like baby elephant trunks, coloured like a papal robe. A quick three hours later and we come to a stop. There is new room for air to pass through the plants, for sun to warm the soil. With luck and a few weeks of half-decent weather, we will have a late surge. Too tired to sow, we resolve to return in the week with autumn seed. Our last job is one we have avoided all summer. Two barrels of comfrey tea have been fermenting for too long. It takes courage to open them, not to reel away from the roadkill stink. The first is thick and nasty, looks and smells like slurry. We rinse the sludge at the bottom of the barrel and I spray it over the transplanted courgettes. The second is clean and clear like a healing miso soup. This goes on the beans. I pull an armful of comfrey leaves to refill a barrel. It will be ready by the equinox, a boost of energy for autumn. We leave laden.

1970. Christopher loves Ray from when he first followed me to Basildon. His relationship with Lesley is more conflicted, though this is mutual. It is as though he's waited for Ray all his life. He's held tight to his Jenkins name like a foundling keepsake. He'd never felt like a Drabble and maybe it was mutual. Ray had been a chief petty officer in the Royal Navy, Christopher is a sergeant in the army. They have the NCO value system born from a hermetic life. As the years pass, they share the same prejudices, the same receding hair. We talk about it, sharing our parents out like sweets. One for you and one for me.

He's my dad, not yours, said Christopher from the start, and it was easy to believe. They have grown to look alike. Think alike. They fear the same things. Christopher has cleaved to him. Then, in '87, I discover the birth certificates that seem to show Ray isn't, after all, our father.

You have to go to see him, I say. He adopted us after he married our mum. Whatever it says, he is still my dad, Christopher says. Unlike me, they have always stayed in touch. They have been close from the beginning, for many years. Christopher has been loyal. A Jenkins, he believes and belongs in the church of Ray and his Pentecostal certainties.

He goes to see him and asks about the adoptions. Ray says he's always thought of us as his sons. But he had put us in a children's home, taken Lesley, named for Leslie Ray, and left. When Christopher and I were teenagers, he wouldn't tell us why he wasn't around. You must never ask me again, he said, and we don't until that night. Now the stunted truth squints in the light. Christopher never forgives him for not being his father. They never speak again.

1992. I never knew Christopher to have a girlfriend. He wasn't interested in girls as a boy, or much in women as a man. They aren't interested in him. It is just how it is. He finds a solace in the company of men that is denied to me. While I chase softness and sex, he yearns for Spartan certainties, a pre-Seventies purity. His first wife was a conductor on the bus he drove. His second, Sue, too. He is solicitous and thoughtful. Their words and their sitting together are childlike. Cooing like kids.

Christopher and Sue have invited us over. It's a first. They always come to us for lunch, tea and cake, a walk on the heath, her high heels sinking into the soft earth. He lives on Thamesmead, around the corner from his kids. It is a huge estate, mostly white, like Basildon. He feels at home. He answers the door holding back a giant Doberman, a thick chain around its neck like something securing a motorbike. It follows us as we sit on the low sofa, knees around our ears, heads lower than the dog's. It stands guard, growls, curls its canine lip. Christopher laughs. He got the dog from a neighbour, he says. They had bought it to protect them, then realised they were all afraid. Christopher had put it in a fight with a champion pit bull in a field out the back. The Doberman won, ripped the other's ear off. Christopher is proud. He is happy. The dog feels my fear. I try to stand, hard with its huge head pressed into my groin. It follows me closely into the kitchen, snarling all the time. We don't stay long. We don't go back.

2000. I am talking to Christopher on the phone. He has been paid off from his job as a bus inspector. The work had suited him. He was organised, officious, it came with a cap which he'd customised so the peak came flat to his face. He sports a sergeant's military moustache.

His bosses had offered a lot of money, he says. Our conversation is going well. He is happy. He has bought a new car and two video players, one for downstairs, one for upstairs so he can watch films in bed. Then I wreck it.

Christopher has three children who live on the same estate. Two boys, a girl with a heart condition. He is very bad at birthdays. He had recently sent his eldest son a card a few weeks late. Chris, I say slowly, you should spoil your kids while you can. Take them into town, buy them toys and clothes in Regent Street. You'll never have this much money again. You and I know how much it means. And you know no one needs a second VHR.

I have gone too far. It has been a long time. I recognise the loudness of the silence. She has a boyfriend, he says of his first wife, finally. They are living well on benefits. His voice is tight with anger now. Sue is indignant in the background. Don't ever dare tell me what to do with my own money, he says. He shuts the phone line down.

The next day I buy and send a card. As ever, the conciliator. I am sorry, Chris, I write, mending fences. Making peace is what I do. Then inexplicably I add a fatal final line. This time, I write, you are wrong. And I lose him. Of course, it seems so stupid now. He stops talking to me. He disappears. It's as though he thinks we're after his cash. Like a fairy-tale miser, now he becomes a hermit.

I let him go. We all get on with our lives.

2008. In the end, of course I can't stand it. I fear something could happen to him and I may never know. I ask someone to trace him, a specialist in people who don't want to be found. It doesn't take long. He is close to where he was, around another corner. I send him a card with my love and phone number, same as it ever was. I ask him to call me, say I need to know he's OK. He doesn't phone but sends a note with his number on.

I ring and catch him cleaning his car. He's a bit busy to talk, he says. I tell him it's too many years since we spoke. He says it has only been two. He says he's happy with Sylvia, who came on the scene when Sue finally left. (She used to drain the bank account, phone him when she was with other men. Sometimes she'd have them make the call. She would return when the money ran out. He always took her back. The abandoned boy.)

Women hot-wired him to unhappiness, this strong man with huge hands (mine looked like a kid's beside his: the only thing I envied). He'd cling on. To Sue and to Sylvia, hold hands all the time. Fingers like bananas clutching hers in his.

Anyway, he says, he has to go. Things to do. He'll call me soon. He'll keep in touch. Of course, he never does.

2011. A cold late-January morning. The phone call comes to my office. I am looking for Allan Jenkins, the voice says, I am from the Metropolitan Police intelligence unit. It is about your brother Christopher.

I breathe in. Slowly. I know I am losing him.

He is in hospital, in Devon, he says. He is very unwell. He thought you lived in Southampton Row [it is Southampton Road], but you are unknown at that address. Normally, the cop continues, we may have left it but my father died from cancer at Christmas so I was determined to find you. He said you were a journalist with the *Guardian* and here you are. Christopher is in Torbay hospital. You need to go and see him very soon.

I take a train the next morning, fated Paddington as always. He is in the stroke ward with other shrivelled, sickly men. Sylvia is there and her sister. Christopher is lying on the bed. He is being eaten alive, there isn't much of him left. He looks like his ghost.

He had been feeling a bit ill for a year, he says slowly. He'd been to the doctor a few times for his cough. They gave him some linctus and sent him away. He didn't think much of it but his legs had swollen on the Christmas drive to Devon. Sylvia's sister had insisted on the hospital. They scanned him with an MRI, found thrombosis and clots in his chest. Also lung cancer, like Dudley. It is too late to operate.

I hold his hand like we did as kids. They are the only part of him that hasn't shrunk. I try not to cry. At least you are back home in Devon, I say. Tears release and roll down his face. Come on, cheer up, says Sylvia. I say I think it is OK to cry. If not then, when?

I don't think Christopher fully recovered from his early childhood hurt. The big man with baby talk. It is as though he has always been slowly dying. From being unloved, unhappy. Now it has fully incubated and finally come for him. His life and ill luck have run out.

When Sylvia and her sister leave, I ask the nurses if I can stay. We need more time to talk. To be together, alone. We don't speak much. We sit in silence, two broken boys 50 years on. We talk a little about Devon, about the river, the farm, our near-mum and dad, about being foster kids, a family.

He drifts in and out. Nods off. He is quiet. The morphine drip grips. I hold my breath and hold vigil. I watch as he fades. He struggles to his feet when it is time for me to leave for the last train. For the last time. I hold him up so we can hug. He barely comes to my shoulder now, my brave six-foot soldier, boxer brother. I hold tight. I whisper how I love him. You are my brother, the last thing he says.

Christopher has a stroke during radiotherapy a few days later. He fights for two days before sliding away. Lesley asks if she can come to the service but Sylvia says no. He wouldn't have wanted her there, or any of them, only you, she insists. She asks if I can pay for the funeral. I ask for a couple of days to see what I can get together. When I call over the weekend, concerned by the quiet, she tells me she 'burnt him yesterday'.

I wonder where his ashes are.

I think most of my life I have struggled with survivor guilt, since I cared for Christopher in the children's home, my nervy, older baby brother, broken in a way it seemed only I could see. I could feel his fragility, knew he needed me. Though on this he was mute.

I regret when we drifted. When we fought. When I thrived and he barely survived. When I was wanted more than him. When hurt slipped off me more easily. When I shut him down, exhausted by the rage, the weight around my neck.

I cut him loose because I was unsure we would make it safe to shore together. I wonder why I didn't try harder. It was just love and care he wanted. Why was it so hard? I was intent on escaping who I was, reinventing myself, but Christopher stuck fast with stubborn integrity.

When he wouldn't let go, I let him go. To drift. To drown. To die. Now there is no way to make it right. So I grow nasturtiums and marigolds, like when we arrived at Herons Reach. When I was five and a half and he was six and a half. In orange-tinted memory to show we were there.

AUGUST 22, FRIDAY. A quick 5.30am pop to the plot to tell it I am going away for the weekend and to check on the transplanted courgettes. They have started to spread, the rehomed chicories too. I have sorted autumn and winter seed and boxed them for Howard but I am mostly here to put in an appearance. For the first time in months there are bare patches of earth and growth is slowing. Time is short. I strip a few peas in time to see the fox sneak up the bank at the end of the plot, like a teenager creeping in at first light. I cut a few leaves for the house while I am away. I see Mary has taken the onions. It feels like a good sign. I hope she is enjoying her runner beans. A last look, a quick goodbye and I am home by 7am. There is work to do and a plane to catch before noon.

AUGUST 29. The box has arrived from Plymouth. I ordered it a few weeks ago, a freedom-of-information request for my records – 10 years in the city's care. I need

to know more facts, to sift reality from uncertain memory.
I am now mining deeper into Devon every day but I can
still feel Christopher fading. I can't remember where he
was. I can't much remember when we were happy: one
or two snapshot images but the memory album is empty.
There is no one left to remind me.

I have spent months preparing myself, or so I thought.
Christopher's death is edging out Dudley, my journal less
now an homage to my father than searching for my
brother. I need to dig beyond the marigolds and here it is.
A plain cardboard box in a plain package, postmarked
my past. Harmless-looking. Innocent, though it should
come with hazard tape. Warning! Contains memory
nitroglycerine. I gorge on my photocopied history at first,
the tale of 'two agile little fellows, both proud of being
brothers'.

Single-spaced, there are hundreds of pages. The writing is 360 degrees: reports from welfare officers, care-
home workers, teachers, doctors, and reports and letters
I wish I hadn't read from Dudley, my foster father.

I came to the childcare department's attention this
time aged four, it says. My family is 'well known to them'.
A hospital had refused me a tonsillectomy because I had
scabies and herpes. They were concerned about infection.
Now so am I. I had known I had rickets and history with
tuberculosis, but here lie unsettling layers of grime, like
rooting through a dead man's belongings, the body lain
alone for years.

Scabies, herpes, rickets, TB. Jackpot. A bonanza,
winning a lottery for the unloved.

Christopher had been brought from Portsmouth, it
says, to live with us at the home Ray had with 'Mrs F.',

who looked after us after my mother left. Christopher must have been with my mother, although we'd been told she had run away, never to be heard from again. There is a letter from Sheila too. She has heard about the TB test, is concerned, asking about me. She has remarried, she says.

Christopher had been operated on for a hernia. He was nervous, withdrawn, the records say. He was very small for his age.

The reports are novelistic, unreal, almost unbearable. The first care-home worker reports we had 'no deep attachment for anybody. There was never a murmur out of the boys for "homesickness" or anything like that'. I can't help but wonder why. On another page another shell explodes: 'There is some doubt as to whether or not Mr Jenkins is the father of Christopher, but there is a remarkable resemblance'. This would be cruel if true. Christopher never fully recovered from his conversation with Ray about our birth certificates.

I can't stop reading my story. It is a fairy tale from another world in another time, happening to another child. Who are these boys? Is Allan/Alan/Peter really me? How did Christopher survive?

It is news. Like a drug, addictive. Compelling like coffee. Until suddenly anxious, I have overdosed. Exhausted, at last I go to bed. It is late. My wife looks worried.

I am at the allotment before 6am. I need peace, positivity; to think about something else. One of the wigwams has collapsed, flattening most of the corn. Even here, structures are unsafe. The heavy metal pole is pulled from the ground, bent out of shape like me. I try to right the wigwam. It is too heavy, a two-man job. I walk through the plot, heavy with dew, disturbing a couple of unconcerned frogs. A mouse runs across the path. It is the dog days of summer. My load lightens, my breath deepens. I breakfast on blackberries, more ready for the office.

AUGUST 31, SATURDAY 7AM. I am meeting Emli, a photographer who's asked to take pictures of the plot. She is a social-media friend. We have never met but I know she is Danish, adopted from a Korean family. There is a connection there. Bill is at his allotment when I walk through the gate, waiting for Costa Coffee to open. I am intent on tidying when Emli arrives, I show her around the site, tell her its history. I show off the Trail of Tears, fully purple-podded now, the beans a shiny grey. I give her leaves and herbs to taste: chervil, apple mint, chicory, sorrel, Danish lettuce. We talk about being brought up as outsiders in the countryside and how it stays with you. She has recently broken up with her partner, she says. She has lost her home and her garden. I pick beans for her to take home, we talk about how colours affect texture and taste. The Tom Thumb nasturtium is perfect now, so I offer her flowers. While I walk her to the tube, I tell her that when she next feels the need to be in a garden she'll be welcome to visit ours.

I return in the afternoon like a wounded animal to a cave. Unhappy thoughts and feelings are looping out of control. My chest a generating plant of pain, I am flooding with anxiety, fighting back infant tears I have no immunity to.

I have decided to grub up the wigwam. We need space for autumn leaves more than we need more beans. I pick off the pods and sort them: thin for eating, fat for seed-saving. I wheelbarrow the vines and weeds away, two trips piled high, leaving a trail as I walk. I pick up the pieces. I pack away the poles for next year and tidy around Mary's bed. There are no signs she has been here, the runner beans hang long and lonely. I hoe the cleared bed thoroughly and rake it. It is ready for autumn sowing. It is September tomorrow.

SEPTEMBER

SEPTEMBER 1. The first day of autumn, probably the last for the tomatoes. The end of the summer. For the past few months, 10 unruly plants in plastic tubs have camped out on the roof terrace like gypsies in a Cotswold village. They're there on sufferance. Not for them the beautiful pots that indicate permanence. These are allotment interlopers, grown from Brown Envelope seed. The bulk of the plants are old-school knobbly Brandywine tomatoes, the sort you'd be happy to find in a grocer's shop in Greece. They have thrived this summer, the hot, dry July helping produce two heavy crops (there is a big bag in the fridge as I write). Now they are over, a few small, greenish fruit ripening too slowly among the curling leaves. Any day now the last will be picked, placed in the sun on the sill. The plastic will be packed away until late spring when I will start making needy eyes at my wife, pleading to let me park my gaudy caravan on her green again. After all, a tomato picked in the sun, with salt in your pocket, proves you're a proper gardener.

1987. A week or so after Ray confirmed he wasn't our father, I ask Lesley if she could discover whether there is someone who might know something of our mother, even have her photograph. I don't want anything else from him, no hard feelings as they say, but I feel he owes us that. Lesley brings me the address of Ray's sister. It seems she and Sheila have kept in touch, meet up from time to time. Many years too late, perhaps, but I'm closer to finding my mother.

I send her a letter, saying sorry to intrude but I hope she remembers us. Is there anything she could tell us about our mother. I write that we don't, I think, want to meet her, but we would welcome news of how she is, what she looks like. Would she have a picture, perhaps from the wedding?

I wait for her answer. Weeks pass, hope fades. She never replies.

Fast forward seven months: 7am one Saturday. I am asleep when the phone rings. It is a call from someone named Susan. I don't know her, she says, but she is Sheila's daughter. Her mother had sat her down, told her a story about her old life, about some children she had left behind. The call doesn't compute, I don't understand. It is early. I don't know anyone called Sheila. Then Susan says she is my sister. That her mum had asked if I might call her. Sheila hopes we don't hate her, she says.

I tell her I'll phone around seven. I need Christopher. This is the call we have waited for. As long as I can remember, I've longed to be held by my mother. Maybe I had lost something when I found Ray, the hope it would work, would calm the child I sometimes hear inside.

Christopher comes over. We make the call in the evening, hear the voice of our mother for the first time in 30 years. I cry, of course. I am wracked, rung out with sobbing. Lost and now found, as the song says. Years of longing and rage released. Relief comes off me like steam on a horse. It would never be as real or overwhelming again.

JANUARY 14, 1954. (Though I am not to know this for 35 years, long after finding my mother): 'I'm not having another bastard in this house,' my grandfather Billy calls down the stairs. It is the night before I was born. My Uncle Mike was to tell me this story too many times. Mike might be fuzzy on when we children lived together, if at all, but he is insistent on this. Billy was back from working in the pub and not happy at the thought of his daughter coming home with another child. Christopher was a year old. Born in a Salvation Army home near Exeter, he was supposed to have been put up for adoption but Sheila had changed her mind. She brought him home. Now there is another one and the thought is more than Billy and his wife Doris can bear.

It is the 1950s, in Plymouth, south Devon, where respectable families don't have two illegitimate children and the women don't hang around sailors in red-light bars or lurk around the city docks. Mike has other stories: of my mother climbing out of her bedroom window to go to Union Street; of Doris dragging her home. There are later stories too: of her jealous husband bursting in when searching for his missing wife; of my mother being in bed with two sailors and her friend while 12-year-old Mike tried to sleep. Where his memory starts to fail is on where the kids are. Were we at least together, I ask him and my Aunt Joyce, but the mist of shame has obliterated their memory, although Joyce, the eldest, says she was supposed to look after me until my mother changed her mind.

SEPTEMBER 3. My fourth plot visit in five days, an unusual frequency at this time of year, but not now to water, rather to keep me connected. I have been frit since reading the case-conference reports. I've rewritten history, maybe all my life, like a Stalin-era Soviet, turning my foster father into Santa Claus and now the care notes are calling this into question.

So I am here, Tuesday morning, another early visit before work, late to sow winter salads. I'm on the ghost bus again, with the half-alive in the half-light. With my bag of seed and hope.

I don't have much time and there are many rows to sow. I hoe through the bean bed, re-rake it until I am happy with the tilth. I cut sticks, cut string, lay out short rills. I place a seed packet next to each row. I sow for autumn and winter – chervil, three types of chard; there is pak choi, chicory, Indian and Japanese mustard. Howard arrives. He is back now summer's over. It is the first day of term. Rose has a new teacher, Nancy a new school. I do light weeding while he waters. We squeeze in shorter rows between the overblown summer salads. He picks leaves. I pick beans. By 9am, we are ready to leave. The seeds are in, it is over to the fading sun and our soil.

I will be back again soon to see how they are doing. There is nurturing to be done.

16.3.59. Parklands care home report on Alan Jenkins, by Mrs D Russell, Plymouth:

'A very charming little boy and very brave-faced if faced with disappointment or reprimanded in any way. He, in his turn, is very fond of his brother Christopher and behaves towards him as an older brother instead of the younger, advising him and watching out for any pitfalls that might come across Christopher's way. He hates to see his brother hurt. His personal habits are excellent. He is overjoyed if he can give a present to those in charge of him. (Generally wild flowers.) Alan takes great care of his appearance and one comes across him washing his hands as often as possible. Progress at school is good and he is very fond of his Mistress. His appetite is good but he is certainly not greedy. Alan will be much missed when he does eventually leave Parklands.'

16.3.59. Parklands care home report on Alan Jenkins, by Miss G Fredrik, Plymouth:

'Alan has a very pleasant disposition, and he rarely gives any trouble. He is very affectionate. Unfortunately he was caught telling a lie yesterday, but that is the first instance of anything like that coming from him, and I hope it will not become a habit with him. He is very generous, shares his things. Unfortunately he cries rather easily.'

I still delight in giving flowers and I still cry rather easily. I wish I was still able to advise and watch out for Christopher but it seems I'd forgotten how.

Case conference 17.3.59. Plymouth:

'We have had these children in ever so many times. Mr Jenkins married Mrs Jenkins and she already had several illegitimate children, whom he adopted.

Christopher is the eldest
Alan – born in 1954
Lesley – born in 1955
Caron – born in 1956

We have had to take the children into the Nursery. Christopher hasn't been in care before; he was living with some of his mother's relatives.'

I am still unsure why reading the records is so upsetting except I never knew I had been in ever so many times, and that Christopher hadn't been with me. I don't believe my mother had relatives in Portsmouth. That wasn't why she went.

Sometimes I think there is a reason memories burrow and hide, not wanting to be found. It's why I stopped therapy. I started when I turned 50, a sustained attempt to understand my 'inner life', but I tired of breaking down walls to the scared boy only to brick him up again at the end of the hour. The transition was often too abrupt, like suffering diver's bends: jumping half a century in 15 minutes on the journey from pyschoanalyst's couch to newspaper office.

SEPTEMBER 7. A celebration of harvest time with an end-of-summer meal. Food from the plot – courgettes, beans, chard, potatoes, herbs, cooked on site. There is no sign of Mary, no evidence she has been here. The still-high sun scatters shadows through the tall plot, throwing the fennel into filigree as I strip the last large wigwam. I feel guilty, as it is still pumping out gold and blue beans at an alarming rate but (as always) we can't keep up. It is time to let go. I lift the poles and strip the pods as a pair of wagtails dance on the wing, intricately, by. A late Red Admiral butterfly passes. Howard arrives as I am wheelbarrowing the waste away. He has brought a cooking pot. I have brought tomatoes. I cut a couple of our courgettes: Italian, ribbed and rugged, grown from Franchi seed. They sit well with the corn and sunflowers in a late-summer surge. Howard lights a charcoal fire, cuts chard and digs a few potatoes. I chop beans and herbs into my hand, hippie gypsy style, like when I lived in a caravan and cooked in a can on a fire outside Glastonbury, aged 17. While the pot bubbles prettily, we add our chilli and oregano. The beans soften, the potatoes too, the colours are Mediterranean. Silence is broken by conkers crashing on the tin roof and the green woodpecker's call. Howard's wife Polly, also a fine photographer, arrives with Nancy and Rose. It's good to see them all together. I hoe the bean bed and Polly cuts string for fresh rills. The girls make elaborate floral displays and divide dried garlic and beans into piles. Polly and I take it in turns to sow beetroot, radishes, chioggia. I save nasturtium seed. We eat summery vegetable soup from paper cups while the woodpecker rat-a-tats from a nearby tree. We grill our last corn over the coals. Here among flowers and friends I am happier. After six hours at the plot, I leave replete, a little healed. Nancy gives me a hug.

SEPTEMBER 8. Another bad dream, more torture, more cutting. I have had the same nightmares as long as I can remember. There are always knives, there are always men hunting me. I don't often die. This was a repeat of a previous dream: the person to be cut, to be killed, wasn't me but a girlfriend. I knew what would happen. She would be killed by someone I knew with a sharpened spoon. The dream ends when she does. So I am here, wide awake in the dark. Heart pounding, adrenalin sick. My first recurring nightmare was when I was aged, I think, about eight: the devil arguing with my parents for my soul. Every night for about a week I was scared to sleep. I couldn't tell anyone. How do you say Satan is a three-feet-tall, three-legged Siamese cat, smart like Shere Khan from *The Jungle Book*, looks like an Egyptian god, has a BBC accent? Night after night, the conversation went back and forth with the cat about to get me, then I would wake. In the end, Mum and Dad won through. The dream didn't return. The hunting nightmare has been ongoing throughout my adult life, on average about once a month. They always catch and often cut me. Always blades. Maybe it's about the closeness of the danger. The dreams are mostly unrelated to the day, seemingly not triggered by stress (yesterday was a good day), but they always come back.

1960. Plymouth and Portsmouth, twin cities of despair, sinkholes of transit, servicing sailors. Beacons of unloveliness, hopelessness and open wounds. When I wondered what happened to my mother, where she was, where she had been, when I trawled Plymouth's streets in hope of finding her trace, Portsmouth should have been obvious, the same vibe, the same vice. In my care records, Christopher's happiness is measured by how much he talks about what happened in Portsmouth, until the darkness lifted. It took a year or more for his fear to retreat, though like a virus it lay dormant. I don't know why I don't remember he came from there. I was four in the children's home but I could see he was hurt, had been snared, was a little strange. He had been marked like a stolen banknote, visible only to people expert at scanning for pain. Exiled from Eden, his childhood hope eaten away. A cancer-causing trauma, etched too deep for me to reach.

SEPTEMBER 10. Denmark. Back at the summerhouse as the migrating birds and other tourists gather to leave. Hedges are alive with chattering starlings, clustering in liquid clouds swooning over the bay; geese criss-cross the sky in squadrons, their anxious calls signalling time to go; the nearby farmer's field has become a temporary home to a large group of cranes, standing tall and motionless like Antony Gormley statues, waiting for stragglers. Their wings stretch out like old people putting on a coat. We bicycle close and watch with binoculars, the kids with us entranced.

It is mushroom season and they have exploded like dandelions: scary scarlet fly agaric are dotted through the plot like Alice's Wonderland. Others are coloured amethyst, violet, murky pinks. Some are like scattered leaves. We skip our special foraging spot and lazily fill a basket with ceps and other boletus in the plantation by the beach. They make a pasta dinner with parsley and garlic. The good neighbour has emptied his eel net and found a couple of dozen crabs. We quickly dispatch them, slow-cook them in wine and water; the broth will be a base for soup. One of our apple trees is still laden with fruit, wasps are feasting on the windfalls. The pears have mysteriously disappeared. There are banks of blackberries on the beach to make pies with apples for autumn.

There are chores to do but most will wait so we cycle through the woods along the shore. There is a warm burst of Indian summer as we laze in the September sun. Some of the trees need attention, a few are dropping branches, looking a little bedraggled, but Bo, the tree surgeon with the missing finger and Viking beard, costs more than we can easily afford. We will cut out a few of the trees ourselves and leave only the tallest and expert trimming to him. Meanwhile, we order a couple of cubic metres of ash logs for Christmas. The trees we chop this winter will warm us through the next.

The fields still whisper summer, Pollocked with ox-eye daisy, cornflower, poppy. We fill a few vases. We are back in a month, when we will gather berries and beach apples along the shore. We tour the garden first thing every morning, admiring the spider webs thrown like fishing nets through the grass, the boletus, primrose leaves already shaping for spring. There is a Nordic winter yet to come but, as in Devon when the last ice-cream van left the beach at the end of summer and we returned to walk the dog along the empty sand, the belonging here deepens as we wrap up warm and dry against the cold and wind and rain.

My first wild food was, of course, blackberries, eaten on the back lane to school. Later, gathered with milk cans and Mum. I don't remember Christopher being there so he must have escaped. Mum disapproved of eating berries before they were thoroughly washed. Cleanliness being next to godliness was one of her core beliefs. I couldn't wait, and couldn't hide my purple shame. Hazelnuts were another hedgerow treat; trying to bite into them, wondering which would break first, shell or teeth. Sometimes the nuts were empty, mostly they were sweet. Christopher could never be bothered but I would fill my blazer pockets.

There were field mushrooms behind the house after Dudley put in dairy cows. I would go out before Saturday breakfast to hunt through the clumps of greenest grass. No one else would eat them. Dad disapproved of things found free. Mushrooms were oddly suspect. The countryside (like Christopher and me) wasn't to be trusted unless tamed; fields were to be worked, planted with fruit trees, red pines, or rented out for animals. I was always comfortable with wildness, Christopher more comfortable with the farm.

SEPTEMBER 15. The roof-terrace tomatoes are still turning red. It is looking as if they'll all ripen. I will pick them at the weekend. The magnolia leaves have coloured and curled, those dropped are gathering in swirls around the pots. We will have to sweep soon. The echinacea flowers have rusted and frayed like battered moths. The geraniums are still brave and strong, as too the tagetes, orange as Sunny D. The dahlias are losing the fight against mildew, each flower more precious now. The impulse-bought chrysanthemum is a glitterball, a disco riot of purple colour (how Dad would disapprove). The pink schizostylis has thrown its arms open, extravagant stems confidently reaching out, demanding admiration. I am hoping autumn will bring birds back to the abandoned feeder. I will switch from seed to nuts, see if I can entice them.

Care report, Plymouth:

Date and time of proposed receipt of child, Friday, 19th day of Sept 1958

SEPTEMBER 20, SATURDAY, 5.30AM. I have arranged to meet Howard to sow at 6am but there is a torrential downpour, lightning. The first text arrives at 5.40am. Howard: 'eating bagel hoping rain stops'. Quite rainy, I reply. 'Feeling like it might be too wet for seeds, can drop them off if you want,' he responds. We message back and forth for another 15 minutes before we call it off. The ground is soaked. The rain doesn't stop.

I head up around 3pm. I haven't been at the plot for a fortnight since the early-autumn sowing and soup.

Everything is falling – apples, unpicked tomatoes, the summer light. It seems we have moved a month in two weeks: misty rain like low cloud hugs the ground. At the plot, two of Mary's weed sacks are waiting patiently to be emptied. She has been clearing the bed by the beans. At least I hope it is her. I will return tomorrow, weed a bit more, but today is just a quick tidy, a chance to say hello. The first sunflower is out, a quiet riot of spiralling seed. The courgettes are growing into marrows. It is like the Seventies. I will wait for Howard and inspiration. I take the easiest option and cut three smaller fruit for a Saturday ratatouille. Slugs are feasting on the squash and chard. I kill a few, throw some snails over the wall (is it only the shell that makes me more kindly disposed?). Some amaranth has been flattened by rain; I cut a long, purple-trunked bunch to take home. The late-summer seedbeds I sowed with Polly look promising, the radish leaves a confident run of green. I will hoe them through tomorrow and pick a small bunch of nasturtiums, jewelled by raindrops. They are a reminder as always, as constant as the quiet gardening brings.

SEPTEMBER 21. Howard picks me up at 7am. Only a day away from the autumn equinox and there is no hiding it now. The plot is slowing, energy drawing back into the earth, but until then we have the marrows. Howard has ideas of a Greek-style dish with lamb; I am thinking something Provençal. My wife will roll her eyes at another sack of unwashed food to find room for. The morning is clear and cool with a heavy dew. There is little sign of summer midge. The nasturtiums are like lily pads, only missing their frog prince. As the light hits the tree tops, I spy a flash of red, an unmistakable profile, my first spotted woodpecker here, bathing in the sun. We watch till it flies off for Hampstead Heath. A squirrel leaps from tree to tree like Tarzan, unleashing a cascade of conkers that takes out others further down. While Howard photographs, stopping only to show me the results he is happy with (it is good to see him with his camera again), I hand-hoe the new 'leaf bed' where the collapsed beans have been. It is precise work, intensely satisfying, evening out the odds against the weeds and other obstacles. The pigeons are already culling the sweet-tasting baby kale and winter salads. We pick late salad leaves and each take two marrows (I cook mine with tomato, onions, garlic, ginger and turmeric for a southern Indian curry). The woodpecker calls goodbye.

I return that afternoon to find Mary, freshly scarfed, looking slight but strong. She has been digging. Her operation has been deemed a success. She is busy hoeing and pulling weeds, talking of shopping for new clothes, maybe a dress. She feels she has more options now she has lost a little weight. There is vigour in her walk and talk, her weeding. We discuss her treatment, our winter plans and the merits of early onions. I am so happy to see her. She picks perpetual spinach and runner beans. I offer to dig her potato patch. It is still too much for her. I turn over the heavy soil in a largely unsuccessful search, digging deeper like an anxious pirate with an unreliable map. After an hour or so, Mary stands me down with six potatoes to show. We may have to revisit our trenching plan. Howard may have to help.

SEPTEMBER 28. No good deed goes unpunished. I am racked in pain and discomfort as Mary does the digging. The wheelbarrow is stacked high with weeds. I can't stand straight. Three days this week I've been pinned to the floor like a butterfly on a board. I am eating anti-inflammatories. Was it just the potato digging that undid me or my care records, perhaps a backbreaking combination? Whatever the cause, I've collapsed and now it is Mary who is revived and working her land while I sit invalided and watch. The sun shines through the thinning leaves, the curious robin is excited by the promise of bounty from Mary's broken soil. I cut herbs and admire the sprawling sunflowers decorated with sleepy bees. My plans are on hold. It seems I need to rest. Sit quietly. Soak it in.

SEPTEMBER 29. 'If I met my mum, I'd have asked, excuse my language, "Why were you such a cunt?"' My mild-mannered, saintly sister Lesley is talking about why she refused to see Sheila when I found her. Lesley is a nurse, a sister on a geriatric ward. She understands a helpless cause. For the past 20 years her life has been immersed in her two boys, Russell and Justin. She has always lavished them with love. Then last year, Justin was hit by a car and killed. Lesley and Justin dyed their hair the same (though Justin told me his was black and red while his mum's was red and black). Lesley is still bitter about Sheila abandoning her. She is a mother. She can't forgive.

I have horror-movie memories of being restrained, strapped down, when I was small. I was young. It was after Sheila. There was another woman I barely remember, though I know the room I was locked in was dark. Family memories are shared and re-shared, part of the architecture of who you are, but what if the memories you carry with you have worn thin and frayed? You have taken them out to read like an old newspaper cutting but how reliable could they be? Until one morning in Camden when my sister Lesley starting talking about crusts. When Ray and a woman he lived with had separated they'd found bits of old bread, she said. Lesley had hidden them under the carpet to eat when she was being kept in a cupboard.

What was it with Ray? Did the Pentecostal preacher have a serial addiction to dangerous women? From frying pan to fire. This all in the Jenkins name I have carried. The one I slewed off only to reclaim it – my pawn-shop identity. Now it's been redeemed and worn with love by those who love me. Here at least, at last, I may have honoured Christopher.

SEPTEMBER 30. I am back in the therapist's chair, the plastic pocket clock facing away, the box of tissues almost to hand. I have been troubled processing the care records. They are too indelible, too true, without the cosy comfort of selected memory honed from storytelling. The records box and the two little boys and their fate torment me – the language used, Dudley's transition from Santa to salesman. A sympathetic face is opposite; we are both in low bentwood chairs. There are cushions on the floor, a small sandbox on the sideboard to help children express their fears through play. It has been seven years since I sat in a room like this. I thought I would never return, but fear keeps coming back like nausea. I am haunted by snatches of ill-formed memories and my dead brother.

The therapist is a specialist in childhood trauma, listening to voices choked by tears, and I try not to cry, honestly, but too often the words and thoughts and feeling overwhelm me. I hide my eyes, my mouth, and reach for the tissues. Yet again my gaudy tale unwraps in faded Technicolor: the tart with no heart, the bullies, the boys. She speaks only to seek clarity: who is dead, who is still alive. I sob, I speak. We agree to start working together next week. After an hour I leave for work. The sadness stays with me.

OCTOBER

OCTOBER 1. Dudley's birthday. He would have been 105 today. He is a colossus in my life, this old man. A therapist once asked why I didn't talk about not having or knowing a father, why it was all about my mother. The question stuck with me. I am aware of my search for acceptance but I had no answer. There had been Ray, of course. He had confused me for a while when he took me in, though I think I had always known he couldn't be, wouldn't be, 'him'. The only answer I have is Dudley, my father figure. My dad. With him, at least, there was something, someone, to aspire to. His love for his wife, his piece of land, carving something from nothing: a house, a garden, and me. He has always loomed larger in my life than Lilian; a little easier to attach to. He pulled me from the abyss, offered me shelter, a life, a home, a name (Lesley still calls me Peter; she is the last one left). I came from 'poor material', he writes in an unsentimental note to child services. This from the man who was a standard bearer against the mongrel masses, who loathed cities and the mixing of race. The reports say he was 'disappointed' in Christopher. More poor material perhaps, unable to transcend his blood and past. Is it possible to love someone and still despise their culling of Christopher's hopes? Within a year of our arrival, the papers say, our adoption was on hold, the requests to Plymouth for more money more insistent. It is hard now to square the meanness, the extreme carefulness with cash. Why should I be troubled by the impatient attempts to get 18 shillings back other than it hurts that Dudley Drabble wanted someone else to pay for Peter Drabble's presents? But compared to the ghost figure who fathered me, the Christian preacher who could never forgive, then I'll take Dudley and wear his colours, if no longer his name. Sometimes there has to be acceptance. Sometimes the searching has to stop.

OCTOBER 4. Driven indoors by incessant rain and melancholy. Autumn has come, the temperature's dropped, the onion sets have arrived, ordered almost without thinking. Every year I toy with the idea of not sowing sets, garlic, early broad beans; not nursing them through frosts, from attacks from predators and wet winter, but by the time the stream of seed catalogues arrives, promising spring and green shoots, my reservations vanish and I am ready to start again. My back is fragile, my heart heavy, but gardening for me is medicinal, an antidote to what troubles me. A friend texts to tell me of her 'deep soulful sadness, like a sinkhole in my thoughts'. She ordered her care records a little before me, so we share this rare disorder. We are both lately overwhelmed by an overdose of information but it is too late now. Unhappiness is trapped inside me; sometimes sleeping, mostly stirring, too often now its wings beat restlessly. Knowledge as insistent as winter rain, distilled into misery. The last element to be released from Pandora's box, they say, was hope. So I will mourn the children we once were and I will sow chicory for bitterness. I will plant spring beans and alliums. I'll look after them.

OCTOBER 5. It's a quiet, sunny Sunday, the autumn air is still, almost holding its breath. Mary is here and has been working through the week clearing the bank and the bottom beds. Sacks of nettles are piled up. We chat for a little while and I carry her weeds away. I'm standing straight but I'm not looking to dig so much as feel out late sowing spaces and my thoughts for the winter plot. Howard arrives. It's maybe the first time we have all been together since spring. The late sunflowers are bunched, two to three metres tall. Branches of orange-tinted hydra heads gather in quiet conversation. Insects hover, fly low and slow as though running out of fuel. The amaranth is backlit velvet, fluffy as a dressing gown. I stuff my jacket pockets with beans from the last late planting, harvest a few courgettes complete with flower I will slice into soup later. I divide my haul with Howard. Sowing and planning can wait another day. For now, I am basking in low sun and a sense of belonging. Plot 29 has wrapped me in its loving magic.

1987. Sheila is a shock. Christopher and I have taken the train together, perhaps for the first time ever. We are in our early thirties but it feels as if we are wearing shorts, evacuee kids in wartime, our names on a plaque around our necks. I almost hold his hand. This is it. Back, finally, to where we started. Susan is waiting at the station, she has the look of Lesley – kind, compassionate, a little confused. The house is on a corner, Paulsgrove estate, Portsmouth.

Then there she is, our mother, standing at her door with a stick. Short, fleshy, her hair dyed raven black, morbidly obese. She sits in her front room like a fat spider dripping in gold and draws me into her web. She isn't what I had hoped for, but I can feel an insistent undercurrent pulling at me, my mother's corrupt connection. Christopher is beaming, bubbly. I feel the first clutch of anxiety, then a lifetime of longing breaks through. The addict has found the pharmacy, dishing out narcotics to the lost and under-loved. We eat sandwiches and sausage rolls. She tells her stories; they sound hollow and over rehearsed. My father had been Scots, a sailor, she says; they had been in love a long time. But I have spun my own fictions, I know when it isn't truth. It can wait until we know each other better. She is my mum. I'm not going anywhere. She had to run away from Ray, she says, taking the baby, my sister Caron, named after Ray's ship. He had threatened to hold her hand in a fire, she says. It's what hell would feel like for the damned and unrepentant. There are to be no tears this time. It seems our first phone call has me all cried out. After a few hours it is over. My brother Michael, the one who looks like me, waits in a car down the road. He won't come in, wary of what it all means. On the train back, Christopher is radiant, bouncing off the walls. I am overexcited, wrung out, aware something is wrong, but I will call her every Saturday night, faithfully forgive.

1992. I am invited to my grandparents' diamond wedding, Billy and Doris celebrating 60 years. I have been adopted into my family. Freed from shame. There had been a reaching out, an invitation to become part of the family I might have had if life hadn't intervened. Uncles were there in numbers, Aunty Joyce, cousins; the Beale clan, their friends. A large room full of strangers, occasional faces with familiar eyes. People come over to me. They cluster. I had lived for a while with a number of them, it seems, looking over me now with sticky curiosity, some sort of concern in their voice. They are seeking recognition. Their memories bubble. Mine stay locked away. We had you to stay one Christmas, one says, though they don't say why, or where my mother was. Another had taken me in for a 'few months' but this isn't the time or place to ask. It is a celebration of staying together. Suddenly, the room goes hush. Something is wrong. I look to its centre. My mother is coming in, slowly, on her sticks. Uninvited and unwelcome. My sister Susan and her husband Jimmy escorting her. No one moves or knows what to do as she edges towards a table. The celebration stops. Sickens. She has greedily sucked its life. The feral ghost in the room. The hideous, hidden secret. I dutifully join her at the table. What else to do? She is my mother.

Sheila is a mystery, clear as mud. I have pored over her pictures, read about her in my records. Sifted my memories. She is elusive. A shy, awkward child at an early family wedding; triumphant, earthy, sexual at her own. Still aged only 20. She and her husband appear mismatched, ill-starred, trading sex for salvation. Ray is here in his navy uniform, grinning, holding Christopher.

Even here she is hard to read, impossible to divine. I may as well cast cards. Was it the war that shaped her? A Plymouth bombsite kid, her mother having a breakdown, her father in a Japanese prison camp. What went so wrong? No way to know when. She had something that drew men to her, other than availability, rarer though that was. Whatever it was it died. She was a shell by the time we met. A host to something dark. You could almost see it lurking, lazy, comfortable, dangerous, in her shadows.

MARCH 1995. I am watching Sunday football on TV when the call comes. It is my sister Susan saying my mother had died from a ruptured hernia while she was in hospital. It is unexpected. She is just 60, but the shock for me is that I am not in shock. I want to feel more, to mourn her but my eyes remain dry, my tears stubbornly stay away. I return to watching Spurs on Sky Sports 1. The next morning on the way to work, I collapse getting off the bus. I fainted, I think, and lie sprawled on the pavement like a beetle on its back. Stunned. I go into work and tell them I won't be coming in. I need time, I say, my mum has died.

I had hardly known her. Hadn't scratched her surface. We had talked mostly about food, about what we were eating, what she was cooking. She craftily steered me away from secrets. Any chance of knowing what had happened and when – and why – has died with her. There is a huge crowd at the funeral: neighbours, family and friends. She was a power in the Paulsgrove community, an elder of her tribe. Ade, another brother, sings. (When

I met Sheila, I thought she had helped heal the hole we had left in her life by adopting Ade and his sister Tina, but it was of course more pragmatic than that.) The song is heartfelt, beautiful, about the perfect love of a perfect mother. Ade teaches singing. He has a voice. It seems everyone cries except Christopher and me. I see his hurt, feel his loss. We are interlopers in the family car. Uncle Mike has come over from Sweden with his Mercedes and its personalised plates. He films all the flowers, records the tributes, until my brother Michael asks me to warn him off. Michael has turned up like a character in *The Sopranos*, in a group of heavy men in heavy cars. They have come to pay their respects, they say, as people came to pay respect to them. I haven't seen Christopher for a long time. He introduces me to Sylvia. She looks like Sheila. He looks like Ray. The next family gathering will be our wedding, he says. The tone is odd. It will never happen. The imprisoning walls between us are too high. Our ladders too short and shaky.

OCTOBER 10, EARLY. Ebeltoft. I was woken by moonlight, like a cop shining a torch on a park bench, but it is cosy firelight inside now. I am back in the Danish summerhouse drinking English Earl Grey tea. We are here to plant tulip bulbs. Unusually, there has been no frost as yet, but autumn is advanced: the grass is flecked with jewelled leaves, copper, old gold, ruby, rust. There are mushroom parasols in the meadow, an occasional stubborn dandelion, herb robert, ragged robin. Lazy, kippered smoke snakes in among the misty trees. The air smells almost sweet like heather honey. Dew pools together on the terrace like splashes of monsoon rain. A seagull passes, lit golden by early sun. Indignant crows call their dissatisfaction. Hedge birds gather by the feeder, disturbed by a jay that walks down the skinny branch to the seed balls like a wary tightrope walker. Spider webs spread on every doorway in a determined bid to wrap the house up like a fly. It is the time of abandoned nests. The blackbird has freed up the woodshed; the climbing rose reveals a front-loading wren's house, hidden until now. We marvel at the intricacy and the idea of offering the tiny bird a family home. A goldcrest, minute as a baby mouse, crashes into the window. We watch, concerned, as it lies stunned for half an hour; its anxious mate swerves late from another pane. The fallen bird recovers and flies away.

Other birds are gathering to leave in swirling flocks. Geese and ducks crisscross the skies. A lone heron flies by: a memory of Dudley and of Devon. The quiet is occasionally broken by the crack of a gun; hopefully the hares are safe. The sun rises through branches of trees I have planted, shaped like happiness. We watch the sunset over the sea. The house is lit by vases of chamomile and daisies, gathered in armfuls from great banks in the fallow fields, a waving sea of white and green in the wind. We eat breakfast outside, basking in mid-October sun. Later, we clear smothering ivy creeping into the meadow. We make room for naturalising tulips. They may take three years but this isn't a goal-orientated exercise. Leaves float in the light breeze like paragliders coming in for landing, catching light like coloured glass. We buy sunflower seed for the hedge birds and strew feeders through the branches like lanterns. Two mice stare at us in the shed. They are preparing for the cold by eating our gardening gloves. They will make a break for the house, though the pine marten will beat them to it. Mist comes in on the last day; the Danish flags in the town hang limply now. The rain, reluctant to leave, settles over the old plantations. The branches drip, the temperature drops. The last pale garden rose of the year holds out till our final morning, petals dropping among the cherry leaves. Winter is coming.

OCTOBER 18. I haven't been to the allotment for a fortnight and it shows. The last bean sticks have collapsed (of course), crushing chicories, their greens turning slimy brown. Slugs and small snails are scattered through the leaves like scouting parties. There is an air of lack of care, of rot and decay, of the sick and dead and dying being dragged beneath the soil. The courgette stems have turned translucent. The leaves are exhausted. The pigeons have battered the late seedlings. The sunflowers are bent like old men. I have to train my eye to spot the stubborn life but it is here, shyer now, less obvious. I strip the velvety cover off the face of fallen sunflowers, marvel at seed patterns. I leave them on the table for birds. I pull the more hopeless plants and take them to the compost; they will return to the soil in the spring. I gather nasturtiums, still spreading, climbing, colonising (their oranges and rusty reds are picked out in the morning screen light as I write). I spot a last corn I have missed and strip it back to its astonishing ruby kernels and silks; it tastes of warm autumn and nuts. I will save the rest for seed, though I already have too much. I pick bull's blood, ochre-stemmed chard, puntarelle chicory, assorted colourful leaves. I will return tomorrow with intent, perhaps with Howard. It is time for an intervention.

OCTOBER 19, SUNDAY. The overnight rain finally stopped, the sun broke through, it is unseasonably warm, nudging 19°C, humid. Ruth and Annie are ferrying buckets when I arrive. One of the water tanks is leaking into Ruth's plot. Their plan to lift the tank is aborted when I point out it is fixed to the stand-pipe and we don't have a screwdriver. They empty the tank and carry on with busying around their plots. A large pile of Jerusalem artichoke stems lie at the top of our path by the pumpkin pit. Mary has been active, a corner has been turned. She is refocused. Renewed. I cut fallen sunflowers and start tidying, moving through the plot, thinning through sickly kale. Some beetroot plants have fallen, their sweet roots eaten away. Mary arrives with her nephew and starts clearing: piling up overgrown undergrowth which he wheelbarrows away. It is a good afternoon, the three women back being active at the industrious end of the site. I like being part of their sisterhood, though they might kill me for calling them that. Howard is still stuck in town buying a raincoat for Rose, so my plans are revised. I rip out the fallen beans and strip them of pods. I'll add the last borlotti to an autumn soup (I can't resist podding a few to reveal candy-striped fruit, like kids' sweets). Three hours fly by. Spaces are opening up. There is still much to do, but for now I have held back the fall, slowed the decay.

OCTOBER 21. Back with the therapist in the room of tissues, sandbox and tears. Halfway through the schedule now, still no nearer or clearer an understanding of why I'm more haunted now 50 years on. What is it I want to know, what does it matter what happened and when? Isn't it enough to know that the more I know, the less content I am? How can a note from a children's home in 1959 unman me? I see Christopher's nervous tic, his twitching, fearful smile. It's not that I think this thing can be fixed; it's not that I cannot 'cope' – though at the moment, I am hurting as if from flu, an insistent, nagging ache. The therapist listens patiently, she makes engaged, insightful comments. But why am I compelled to keep waking up as though in a piss-wet bed? I had thought gardening had freed me. And truly more than whisky, food, sometimes even love, it speaks to me of healing and happiness. I am concerned, I think, that somehow my past is a burden from which I might never be free.

OCTOBER 23. I lose myself for a few hours in the morning. The amaranth is fallen, its deep crimson colour contrasting with amber conker leaves, vivid green chicory, chocolate-cake soil. The late French radishes are crisp, plastic pink. I am joined by a curious magpie intent on stealing birdseed; a blackbird scurries past. I think I may be more at home here than anywhere. Perhaps Plot 29 is a feeling more than a place. There is belonging here on my own, hoe in hand. My mood subtly shifts as quiet steals over me. I used to think it was all about Dudley but whether it is nurture or nature feels less important than growing peace here with potatoes.

OCTOBER 24. Devon, Aveton Gifford hill, the one I used to race down on my racing bike overtaking nervous cars. They have widened the road now, the banks are steeper, I can't see the house from the crest. We cross the bridge over the Avon, take the sharp turn on to the tidal road, turn the corner and there it is, set back from the river, North Efford, known by us as Herons Reach, nestled into the hill. I have passed by here, slowly, a handful of times since I lived here but I have never stopped. Today is different. I turn off the road and through the gate, past the squat, shale stone barn, the drive to the house paved now, not gravel. The apple trees are twisted, gnarled and lichened. The planting has matured, the garden has been Gullivered. It's closed in and spread out, like me. I walk down the steps to the front of the house. They feel too small. I have run up and down them a thousand times. I need to re-orientate and adjust my sight. The porch has been glazed into a small conservatory. I knock on the door, there's no answer. I knock again. Windows are open, there is bedroom light but no sound. We are close now but still no answer. I feel my anticipation leach. I walk out on to the riverbank. It feels odd to be in the garden. A white egret flies lazily in, like the herons of my day. I wonder where it's come from. The familiarity shimmers, becomes fragile. I am standing deep in my childhood here – T-shirt and shorts, always blue for boys, fishing net in hand.

Here is where we had our rowing boat. The bank was home to Nelson, the one-eyed swan; over there the rushing, hissing geese that guarded Josie's gate. Round the corner I would wait for the kingfisher on the bank by the quiet eddy, hours coloured by an iridescent second. But the river has shrunk. There are new mudbanks with reeds. The wobbly stepping stones where we would cross if it wasn't too deep have been replaced with boards and sturdy blocks; Lilian, pewter hair freshly done with her shopping, would gingerly feel her way across while we surefooted boys skipped over like goats, only very occasionally falling in.

A melancholic mist has come down now, insistent drizzle blurring the boundaries between times. It feels like a lifetime since I stood here, this place where I discovered family, the animal joy of running free. Someone is coming down the steps to talk to us. She has a politely anxious look. I tell her I spent a happy childhood here, point out the trees we planted, the flower beds, though there are no more nasturtiums now. She tells me she has lived here 30 years. Her daughter's three-week-old baby is in the parents' bedroom, her 90-year-old mother in mine. She asks us in for tea. I walk over the threshold for the first time in more than 40 years. I am almost tearful – fearful – now. There is the small window seat almost carved out of stone, where I sat reading Robert Louis Stevenson, looking out over the river for my cat Tuppence coming home, watching out for white owls, like spirits, flying by. We sit for an hour, urgent memories flooding back. Of farm boys, now like me, old men. I can hear James driving the tidal road on his tractor. Names I had no idea I knew bubble up from memory mud: Josie had just died, Frances married a Tory MP, Tina still lives at Icy Park, Richard is running his dad's farm by the church. Continuity is easier in the country, though the ceiling beams are lower than I remember. I stoop into the sitting room where we watched BBC, where I read to Lilian's mum, where Dudley failed to follow through with beating me for making a hole in the hedge. This is the house of hope, of Christmases and birthdays and endless summers, of raking grass and sowing seed, the place I learned to be a boy. Sticklebacks and eels, cockerels crowing, the dog fox walking past the bedroom window, the donkey I could never quite get to Bigbury Bay, all here in my safe place, the Plot 29 prototype. But here, too, lurk darker memories – of the predator neighbour and the family member who abused me. I wonder now what signals they read, like Savile. Was there maybe a mark I carried that let them know I wouldn't tell? Was it because I smelled of foster child? Did they molest my brother? Does it matter now they too are dead or even older men? The boy they touched perhaps forgives but can't forget. My tea is cold; it is time to go.

I feel a familiar wrench, a tug on my sleeve, as I leave the house, past the porch where Lilian podded peas, down the drive where the fading ghost of Dudley smiles in his RAF beret, his grass-stained cords, past the croft where Christopher laughed and we played cricket. All gone. I won't be back. But Herons Reach, returned now to its old Devon name of North Efford, has happy memories still to share, perhaps with the baby behind the bedroom window.

OCTOBER 26. I never took to Horswell. It wasn't the house's fault, but a small cluster of cottages was tough after the river's solitude, and it never felt like home. Dudley's plans to downsize were too obvious. There were too many arguments, the threats to send us back to the city too often said, and too easily. The spell had been shattered, the safety bubble burst. Puberty was a disappointment for everyone, a war between Lilian's anger and our raging at the changing of the rules. Alan Jenkins didn't exist any more and Peter Drabble was confused. After 10 years together, I had forgotten that love must be exhaustingly earned every day like a salary. Enthusiastic gratitude was the only default. My pass needed daily renewal. My name change could be revoked at any time.

The best thing about Horswell was the beach. South Milton Sands was half a mile away at the end of the narrow lane. I loved its teaming life in summer, the worldliness holidaymakers brought with their cars, their bikinis, but it was the winter I loved best. The last, fast-draining dregs of family were here, when we would walk to the abandoned beach with Tessa and let her run: her old-lady, Old English Sheepdog hair streaming behind her in the sea wind and fading light. Our life together was fragile now; being at boarding school hadn't worked, wasn't near enough. Christopher was in the army. I felt alone, like on a lilo, drifting in mist, out at sea.

The last time I was here I was 15 years old, a year after being exiled. I wanted to come home. I'd hitchhiked. I wanted my mum and dad. I didn't fit in Basildon; my school was full of skinheads with Dr Martens boots. Me in shaggy hair and ragged espadrilles. I didn't make it through the front door. Dudley let me sleep in the conservatory. Mum was in the garden when I woke. It was early. She was burning my patched Levi's in a garden oil drum. She said I could maybe stay a few days but first I needed to cut my hair. It was touching my shoulders now. We drove towards Kingsbridge but pulled into a gate two miles outside. I couldn't be seen looking like that with my father, said my mum. So I walked the last bit on my own. My first trim wasn't short enough. I was sent back for another cut. After, Dad took me to the local outfitters while Mum did her shopping. He bought me blue cotton trousers, a coloured shirt. It felt like a breakthrough. The next day I talked about my plans to go to art college in Plymouth. They told me I couldn't stay. It was too much to ask. It was over. There was no going home, no going back. The new haircut and clothes weren't enough: I might look the same but I'd somehow mutated. They would refuse to see me for nearly 20 years. In my Plymouth care records lies Dudley's irritated note, impatient to be reimbursed for my haircuts and clothes.

Today I still know every twist of every narrow lane, every steep turn, every passing place, every barn or house before it appears. We pass by the cottages where we lived; there's nothing for me here. Then we are on the beach where the Thurlestone stands in the sea, hunkered down. There are families, wrapped up warm, kids with nets and buckets, rock pools and sand. I can see over to Burgh Island, Bigbury Bay, the mouth of the Avon. A packed cafe offers Sunday brunch, no longer the wooden shack where I sold sandcastle windmills and striped windbreaks, 'Hey Jude' playing on the transistor. I walk a while, commune with memories, watch kids shrimping, but I am soon back on the train to Paddington, the one I took to meet Lesley, breaking the last, worn thread of the Drabble bond. Caterpillar Peter Drabble morphing into Peter Jenkins, butterfly species as yet unknown.

NOVEMBER

NOVEMBER 1, SATURDAY AFTERNOON. It's time to turn the window boxes. It has been oddly warm for weeks, the hottest Halloween ever. The geraniums have hung on. They are flowering but November is here now. The house steps are covered in dried sycamore seed – helicopters we called them as kids. The roof terrace needs refreshing. The tomato plants have curled up as though sleepy; dry-leafed and darkened. Miraculously, there are still fruit. The summer pots are overdue for packing away or replanting, the annuals are over. We have daisies, primulas and baby-face violas to put in their place. Leaves need sweeping, the magnolia is budding. Later, I head to the allotment. It has been a fortnight since I was here. Annie's swapping plots to somewhere with better sun. Mary's here, too. The bean wigwam is down and she is clearing space for green manure. Our sunflowers are finished, the courgettes exhausted; it is time to tidy here too. There are radishes to eat and nasturtium flowers to pick. They are climbing, spreading spots of bright colour, the banks are full of them now. They have outlived the dahlias but their days are numbered. Soon there will be frost.

NOVEMBER 2, SUNDAY. A night and morning of heavy rain has me hunting out the waterproofs. I am working on two fronts: labourer for the roof terrace, humping heavy stuff up the stairs, and doing much the same at the allotment. It is clearing time. I will miss the amaranths' astonishing colour, their exotic heads like twisted trunks. Sown as part of a salad selection, they are allowed to run riot in late summer.

The birdfeeder swings. The young magpie shrieks amused defiance as it steals the blue tits' seed. I pull overgrown chicory sprawling greedily around. Howard hoes. Colourful wheelbarrow load after wheelbarrow heads to the compost, Mary's weed sacks to the wheelie bin. It is mild, the air comforting, forgiving. The site is quiet. We don't talk much. After a couple of hours, the allotment looks as if it's had a haircut, gone its rebellious expression. I am home in time to lug wet sacks and window boxes down the stairs. The roof terrace, too, is clear; the windblown leaves, the annuals and tomatoes are gone. The winter violas and pink daisies wink.

NOVEMBER 4. My fifth therapy session. I need to make a decision. One week left unless I sign for more. The care record anxiety has calmed but left unhappiness antibodies, a smouldering need to know more. Processing the Plymouth information will take tears, and years, to digest. I don't know if I believe it does any good but it seems I am committed.

It was always kindness, not cruelty, that undid me. Was this the secret the sexual predators knew? My search, I think, is for acceptance. Mine, not my mother's; there was nothing there with her, a dark emptiness, a void. I had thought I had found peace. I have taken the cure, surrounded my life with love, wrapped myself in it, luxuriated, shared it as best I could. I found another love, too, hidden at the plot, among the leaves and flowers. I unearth it when I weed, when I sow and when I grow. Nurture and nature live there but still lingering is a need to talk it out, in a quiet room, with a clock and a box of tissues.

12.11.58. Telephone interview with Mrs F. Rang re Alan Jenkins, he is very ill, went into hospital to have his tonsils out yesterday and hospital asked her to remove him, as he is covered with scabies [*another word redacted here*] could we help. Told her we could not admit a child in care with scabies, suggested she went straight away to Dr Nils who would most likely admit Alan to isolation hospital.

14.11.58. Application for reception of children into care of the children committee. Mrs F cannot manage the children.

2001. Uncle Mike has been in touch: my grandfather, Billy, has died. Doris would like me to come to the funeral. The tough old boy has passed away. I am happy for the invitation. The bastard boy redeemed. Billy had outlived Sheila, my mother, his daughter. She has been dead now for six years so I will be representing her and my brothers and sisters.

I am in Billy's backyard, waiting for the funeral car: Uncle Terry is squaring off against Aunty Joyce's husband. There has been a slight, it seems. Two men nearing their seventies with raised fists and voices. Break it up, I tell them. It's Billy's funeral. I go back in to talk to Doris. She is shrunken with age and shock. She says she is glad I came.

We arrive at the service to a Burma Star guard: proud old men who share the same battle scars and survived the camps. There is a soldier recital, the flag lowers, an honouring of one of their own. I cry, of course. The vicar gets up to welcome us: we are here to remember Billy, he says, proud father of five children: Joyce, Terry, Tony, Colin, Michael … except Billy fathered six kids: four sons, two daughters. One is missing. Sheila has been written out. If she doesn't exist, then why am I here? It is the funeral of Billy Beale, scion of the family, whose eyes and mouth I share; an end-of-pier boxer with a thousand bouts and one last fight left. At the death. To the death. The shame of Sheila.

As I stand in the car park outside, my uncles come to console me. We told her, they said, after she put the notice in the paper that didn't mention your mother. Don't do that at the funeral, we said, you know you have invited Allan.

Family I don't know mill around, look sideways at me. Sheila's boy, their curious eyes say, scanning me like a suspect parcel. I feel an ancient sadness, for my mother, for proud old Billy and Doris, unprepared or unable to forgive. They look like me, the Beales: Welsh blooded, Devon born, the same blue eyes I have passed down, but I don't belong here. The hurt was indelible, the history we share scorched.

Then Doris smiles. Coming in the family car, she says? We hug. There is a nice spread, she says. After all, this is Doris's day. She is burying her husband. Like Bill Sikes' dog, I follow.

NOVEMBER 9. Almost balmy, late sun shining through the skeletal trees, stubborn leaves only left. The willow at the high end is gilded by low light. I am talking to Mary. She is here more than me now. We are standing by Don's memorial spot with the ferns in the hollow by the fruit cage. We are talking winter plans. Mary has been busy: she has already planted onion sets and has a bag of green manure. She wants the elder cut back; it is taking too much of her sky. We will wait for the leaves to drop so we can see what I am up against. We talk a little about planting trees, knowing you might not be there to see them mature. I talk about the birch at the summerhouse, she tells me about returning with Don to his family farm, the joy of rounding a ridge to see a group of tall trees his dad had planted there. I am off to Australia in a couple of days and Mary asks whether I will be buying seed. She tells me to look out for a company called Yates. I tell her I can't seem to stop buying seed even though we have enough for several sites; it is about collecting hope – at £2 a packet – I say. She smiles and says that since she has been ill she buys seed because it has a future.

19.11.62. The foster parents have had a lot of expense during the last few years and do not feel they can afford to adopt the brothers at this stage as was suggested when this case was last reviewed.

NOVEMBER 23. Melbourne. I am meeting with Colin Beale, my mother's brother, who has lived here more than 40 years since he left the RAF. We are talking about the care records and, I keep hoping, his memories of my mother. He seems disturbed about the case notes and asks whether I have told other family members. Colin is the family alpha male with his grammar school grades (better than Michael and Joyce's, he says) and a car dealership. He once promised to share 'secrets' about Sheila but he has never been able to deliver. When arranging this meeting for Sunday, my last day in Melbourne, I apologised for intruding on a family day and he asked if I had forgotten I was family. We have the same blue eyes, he says, the Beale mouth, but somewhere in this concept of family, of how to behave, I have hit a barrier. Years after Billy and Sheila's death, I fear the Beales are closing ranks.

He tells me Ray had been around 'from the beginning', that he'd always thought Ray was Christopher's father. He had babysat Lesley, he says, but has no idea where we boys were. The last time he had seen Sheila was when she visited him in hospital just before he went to Australia. I ask if he has any happy memories of my mother. I say all I have is horror. He says he has nothing more for me but he has the name of a song I should listen to. The lyrics of 'Nobody's Child', he says, might help. He waves away more questions. I should listen to Lonnie Donegan.

The words are saccharine sentimental, but easier perhaps for him to empathise with than his family's forgotten boys.

I was slowly passing an orphan's home one day
And stopped there for a moment just to watch the
   children play
Alone a boy was standing and when I asked him why
He turned with eyes that could not see and he began
   to cry
I'm nobody's child, I'm nobody's child
I'm like a flower just growing wild
No mommy's kisses and no daddy's smile
Nobody wants me I'm nobody's child
People come for children and take them for their own
But they all seem to pass me by and I am left alone

Lonnie Donegan, 'Nobody's Child'

NOVEMBER 25. Back in the Kentish Town room of tears. There is a child's pink, heart-patterned blanket next to the sand box. It is the last of the six sessions but I don't appear to be done with it. A talking cure, a coping thing, who knows? I am still unsure why it matters so much now. Is it fear any answers will die with Ray or my uncles' generation? Why can't I bring myself to say it is my story, not a history of what happened to 'the boys'? Why can Colin remember the words to a 1950s song but not where we were while he babysat my baby sister?

Lesley is the last of the people who call me Peter. Christopher was the constant. When Lilian and I would speak every week, I put on that old persona, slightly worn but serviceable. We settled comfortably into weekly calls after not talking for so long (it would not be profitable to meet, her letter had said many years before, when I heard Dudley had lung cancer). My being a successful journalist had helped when we met again; their efforts finally seen to be paying off. Dad was editing the parish paper, they had moved deep into South Milton. Mum didn't drive and he wanted her nearer her friends in the WI, to be enveloped in the village. We were careful about what we said, steered clear of politics, our sense of family still too weak to mention their coffee-table copies of *This England* magazine, their patriotism proudly on display. They moved into – and quickly out of – an old people's home. Dad didn't want to die there. They rented a bungalow overlooking Salcombe, where they would sit in the picture window watching life pass on the river. At 89, he bought the better place next door (it's for your mother, he said, when I asked why). He died just short of 90 and I was convinced she couldn't survive. She was frail at his funeral, unable to stand. Slumped in the car on the long drive, stuck behind a tractor, to the cemetery.

She eked out another five good years. Sitting in his chair, shakily pouring tea. We were close in the last days. On Sundays I would call her (my other mother's call was Saturday night, after she had watched Cilla Black's *Surprise Surprise*). It is Peter, I would say when she picked up the phone. Cards were signed Allan Peter, echoing the name change Dad engineered as soon as Christopher and I moved in (I never discovered the problem with Allan; maybe it was an ownership thing, like renaming a rescue dog). I missed a Sunday call once. She was very upset, this strangely strong yet fragile woman who had cast me out for decades, a near-biblical oblivion for a confused 15-year-old. I quickly apologised. I cherished the careful rebuilding of this fragile family bridge. She was my mum,

Sheila my mother. I loved her. Perhaps we both needed the forgiveness that came with the calls.

With Lesley it is different. I have only ever been Peter to her, the blue-eyed brother she never knew, invading her cosy home, fighting for her record player. An odd country kid with a soft Devon sound butting up against her Essex edge. Hair longer than hers, in search of edgy girls and plastic shoes. She made room in her life and home for me. It must have caused confusion. I was there for about a year, 1969, a source of fascination to some of her friends, a hippie kid with his skinhead sister. We drift in and out of each other's lives, a card, a visit, a phone call. She wasn't interested in Sheila and I almost envied her that. Ray had never talked about her mum. She was insistent on not meeting Sheila or her siblings. When our mother died, Susan gathered together a free-ranging photo album of Sheila, Susan, Mandy, Caron, looking alike: same shape, similar hair, same smiles. Peas from the pod. I took them to Lesley, laid them out on the floor. A Kodacolor bag of absence, framed in smiling family snaps of the childhood she was denied. Lesley started crying, a keening sound from deep. She curled on the floor with the photos. I have carried the guilt of it since. Years later she hosted a family gathering when even Michael came: six siblings with the same scar tissue (it was during the time Christopher had disappeared). Still there at Doris's funeral, when Joyce told us about the 'backstreet abortion', my mother's other pregnancy that came between Lesley and I, explaining why we were born 18 months apart.

The last time I saw Ray was at my sister's house 30 years ago. Lesley was in a relationship with a Palestinian surgeon. He was cooking. We were joined for dinner by Ray and his scarlet-booted woman friend. It was going mostly well – except when Ray said Labour was the party of the Antichrist, the pastor had told them. At the end of the meal, while Lesley was washing up, the friend leaned over to say something about 'people coming here taking our jobs'. I pretended not to hear. Minutes later she repeated herself. I sighed. I told her she was in my sister's house. She was eating her food. It seemed rude. I had tried to ignore her comments, I said, but I wasn't sure he was keeping other surgeons out of work. The conversation ended. The last link of my relationship with Ray was broken. There was nothing more there. Today, though, after reading the records, I fight an urge to turn up on his doorstep, beg him to tell the truth: about what happened to Christopher and me. Was he Chris's father, what was Sheila's appeal, how could he keep a house-keeper who couldn't keep house, how did I come into contact with TB, scabies and herpes?

NOVEMBER 30. A sunny Sunday afternoon, strangely mild at 12°C. The sky is clear, the brightest blue, squirrels are performing circus tricks, leaping from skinny branch to branch. The mustards are flowering yellow, wild Tuscan calendula, too. The Castelfranco chicory is firm and flecked with red. The jagged hedge of puntarelle is still standing tall. I wish I knew what to do with it – make risotto maybe. I am jet-lagged from Australia, gathering winter salad in a daze. The late radishes are crisp and hot so I share them with Mary, Annie and Ruth. As usual, they are the only people here. Howard arrives. He hoes. We have both walked over the heath and enthuse about the leaves on the beech. There is yet to be a frost. Mary's garlic and broad beans are bright yellow-green with life. I wonder if it is too late for ours. Annie is frying sausages on her new plot and invites us for hot dogs. There is red wine in tin cups and a chocolate bar for pudding. The women talk about growing food, late autumn, sickness. Mary says the allotment is healing her, I say I feel it too. We share the last sausages. We empty the wine, I bask in the last of the sun and their company.

We tell ourselves stories in order to live …

Joan Didion, *The White Album*

DECEMBER

DECEMBER 2. The first session of a new series with the shrink. People talk of their 'inner child' as though he or she is a gurgling toddler, natural, like entering Narnia. But what if he or she is a frightened thing, anxious to escape? Sometimes his anger engulfs me: I rage with his voice like in *The Exorcist*. I am learning (I hope) to recognise the signals, to step away before I have laid waste to a friendship, said the unsayable. Gardening swaddles my anxious boy in a basket, sits him in the sun, surrounds him with blackbird song, a soothing nature Norland nanny. There are no fingerprints in the therapy sandbox today. She gently asks, would I like to use it? Adults also act out what happened to them, with dolls, she says. I decline. Baby Allan stays inside, sleeping, for now.

My memory is like flypaper. It catches passing buzzing thoughts and sticks to them as they die. Early memories are mostly built for us by mums and dads, if we have them, maybe siblings, sometimes friends. 'Do you remember when?' is how our story is shared, the way we learn to become ourselves through knowing where we belong. There may be other memories we don't want to believe.

She was my mum, he was my dad, it couldn't have happened. Could it? You mustn't remember is the mantra, the secret part of our private life. Some people excel in spreading amnesia. They spray it around like a fairy-tale spell. They deal in darkness, write invisible chapters, read our unwritten book. Here we have no hiding place. They know who we are before we do.

1963. Tuppence is my Devon cat, big and bold, black and white, from the farm tom crossed with Tonka, our Siamese. My first ever living thing, he is mine alone to love. He comes and goes when he pleases. He leaves mice, rats and birds as a calling card. Once my mum found a weasel lying next to him; Tuppence's flank was torn open. I was anxious until he recovered in a box in the shed with his stitches. Tonka is posh, beautiful, stand-offish at times, too keen to avoid my over-eager strokes. She likes to lie in the sun with her son, curled up together like yin and yang. I relate to Tuppence's heritage, take pride in his size, his mixed blood – a semi-wild dad and more refined mum. I see him on the other side of the river. I wait for his insistent call. One day he catches cat flu. Dudley keeps him locked in the shed. We aren't allowed to see him. So of course I do. I tell him how I love him. I stroke his matted coat. I don't close the latch properly, at least that is what Dad says. I never see him again but for years I imagine a ghostly flash of black and white in the riverbank grass.

5.12.58. Interviewed Mr Jenkins. Enquire about Alan. Mr Jenkins was taking him to the doctors and he was going to have his tonsils removed as soon as his general health improved.

1963. Boy Blue is our donkey. I like to feed him wild flowers, clumps of grass and carrots. He lives in the field behind the house, pretty much undisturbed. We have a saddle but he isn't much for riding, resistant to anything but eating his way along the lane. Bigbury beach is three miles down the river but I never get him there. My plan is to rent him for rides but Boy Blue has a mind of his own. He isn't a horse. He walks slower than me, no matter how much I urge him on. I am never quite comfortable with riding him. I prefer that we walk together, bridle loose in my hand. I get him as far as the golf course a couple of times, at the top of the bay, but the last stretch always seems too steep. I beg a bucket or large bowl of water, he drinks and we turn happily home. I'm not sure I could ever really hire him out for donkey rides. We have a Dartmoor pony in foal for a while. I watch the baby being born, shuddering miraculously, shakily standing on its feet, but Dad soon sells them on. As we grow older, Boy Blue is left alone except when Christopher and friends throw sticks and stones. One day, Boy Blue butts him against the barn wall and bites him on the chest. Christopher screams. I laugh. Dad comes running. He punches Boy Blue in the face. The old donkey lets go. Dad soon sells him to a family whose daughter is going away to college, leaving her pony lonely. I like to think he leads a happier life.

DECEMBER 7, SUNDAY. Nursing a brutal hangover, I finally get to the allotment at the second attempt, late afternoon. The dim light is already fading. A few nights of icy frost have finally culled the nasturtiums, their dead tendrils barely holding on to the bank like fingers letting go before a fall; so much dead seaweed now washed up on shore. I am feeling a need to sow stuff, although it is insanely late. Procrastination planting. Annie has chard seed under a cloche so I am not the only one. The shed mice have been at the broad beans, so they'll have to wait until spring. They have also wrecked many of the onion sets. I am almost relieved. I feel guilty as I push garlic cloves into the freezing soil. Only a month ago, the earth would have still been almost warm. I plant Radar onions, three rills up to the neck, with another thinly covered as an experiment. My hands are bone cold. I have never got on with gardening gloves, feeling the need of soil through my fingers. I hope the alliums are tougher than me. It is almost dark when I leave but winter solstice is only two weeks away. Light will slowly lift, a new year, new growth will begin. Meanwhile, it is home to nurse my hangover. I am in anxious need of chocolate.

1957. My earliest memories are wrapped around Christmas, one with my mother, one without. In both I am aged nearly three, I think, a month before my birthday. Memories feel too young for four, maybe too old for two. In the first I am walking with my mother. I am on the outside, on the left, I cannot see her face but there is a solid comfort to the shape whose hand I hold. A large, lit Santa Claus is on the wall in front of us, a low ledge on our right. I know it is Plymouth. I know it is her. I don't know how I know. Later, aged 16, when I trawled around Union Street, I wondered if she was still there, sitting in a seedy pub or club. She'd have beehive hair, perhaps be one of the prostitutes walking the same streets. It was strangely reassuring. My second memory is of the same Christmas but I don't think my mother's there. I am sick, I think with chickenpox. I cannot leave the room. I have been farmed out to a friend. It doesn't feel like family. There are Christmas cotton wool snowflakes stuck on the windows, as though to compensate: the inconstant comfort of strangers.

1959. Our first Christmas with Lilian and Dudley, they also disappear. We never know where; they never say. We are too young to understand. We stay with kindly friends of theirs who give us cowboy clothes with shiny guns, holsters and hats. Mum and Dad don't do festive. Giving doesn't come easy. Christmas means a matching sweater, maybe handkerchiefs, though there is also Meccano we aren't really trusted to use. Toys more likely come from welfare visits, though Dudley is keen on Matchbox cars. A social worker brings a plastic bag with a fort and soldiers, farm animals bent out of shape from overuse. Others are made of lead, missing limbs, war-torn. There is a peeling, painted three-legged goat. All unwanted except by Christopher. He dotes on them, plays with them all the time. I am less convinced. Then comes the year of the bike. Christopher is desperate, all the kids his age are. Come morning choir, the other boys show off shiny red racers with drop handlebars, five gears, maybe ten. Chris's present is second-hand, a sit-up-straight lady's bike retouched in old green. I feel humiliated for him but he rides it everywhere. I have never figured out why Mum and Dad were so mean with money. On my desk today is Dudley's note asking to be reimbursed for his son's £2 bike plus a small pot of paint. He had a respected job as a registrar, they rented out the caravan and the house extension he'd had built next door. There were thousands of battery chickens in the barn. New cars were bought for cash but birthdays and Christmas were an inconvenience to be reclaimed. Sometimes I can't forgive them the cash or their disappointment.

1964. I am aware my writing has taken a melancholic turn, so perhaps it is time to share a sunnier story. I am aged about 10 (I hope it isn't more). It is hot. I am keen to swim in the river but Lilian is reluctant to buy me trunks. I wonder why I didn't just swim in summer shorts, except from fear of her anger at the washing (she was a bit fixated on her Bendix). Mum and Dad never swim or go to the beach in summer except once with Mum at Bantham Bay, looking at rock pools early on. Mum is always buttoned-up. I have never seen her arms. Female bodies are a mystery to me but I am obsessed with a girl who sunbathes by the river with a couple of other village kids. She is about 14, with long blonde hair, a chequered pink bikini. I yearn to lie close to her in Speedos like Sean Connery. Mum knitted my swimming trunks. They are pale blue, slightly loose, not the sophisticated look I was hoping for. It is never going to work. Bikini girl doesn't swim but the others do. When the tide is high enough, I join in. My trunks fill with water. The thick wool swells. They bend, they buckle, they gape alarmingly. Water pours between my skinny legs. I anxiously clutch the string at the waist to stop them sliding off. She turns over, looks at me. The other kids laugh. Humiliation complete, I scuttle back to Herons Reach.

DECEMBER 14, SUNDAY MORNING. The allotment. Likely my last visit before Christmas. The nasturtiums are a dull, icy sludge. The hungry pigeons are stripping the chicory they have left till now. The soil is crusted with frost. It is mid morning, mid winter, it is gloomy, the only warmth the colour on the curious robin's chest as it sits watching me from the elder. I can almost feel the onions' chill but there are clumps of bright green chervil and new fennel fronds. Flashes of calendula flower look like head-lights seen from far away. I leave a Danish Christmas beer on a few friends' plots and give a present and card to Howard.

1961. Tessa is our Old English Sheepdog. I love her and her big fluffy feet. Christopher isn't so sure, and as she gets older she knows. She arrives as a black and white ball. We are both small. I play with her all the time. My happiest times are when we walk with her, down lanes, across cliffs, along the beach, Dad striding ahead, swinging his stick, Mum with me. Christopher always lingers at the back. He doesn't 'get' walking, preferring to be on his bike, anywhere but where we are. We avoid beaches in summer, too many tourists clogging the lanes, so cram into the little Fiat, two boys with a massive dog in the back, and crawl up the Devon hills to Dartmoor. There is something magnificent about the carpets of heathers, amber bracken, moody tors and granite streams. We might stop at Widecombe or Dartmeet. There might be an ice cream cone or wafer, an occasional cream tea. I love to see Tessa run, but winter is best for that, down by the Thurlestone, racing along the sands. There is another sheepdog at the farm. I have to step over him in the passage at the side of the house as I drop off the milk churn in the morning and pick it back up after school. The dog bares its teeth as I step over it in my shorts. Tessa growls at Christopher, I am not sure how it starts. It amuses Dad, it confuses me. I love to lie with her, snuggle into her woolly coat, but she guards against Christopher.

1970, CHRISTMAS DAY. Aged 16, a little scared of London after sleeping in derelict buildings and parks, I am now living in a grubby bed and breakfast in Plymouth. I share a room with a chef in his twenties who noisily wanks most nights. Barred from the house after 9am, I hang around the bus station Wimpy Bar, talking to girls and to other drifters (derelicts the term at the time). Breakfast, as always at the B&B, is a fried egg sitting in a pool of fat, sliced white on the side. It is Christmas morning so today there is a bottle of beer. I don't like beer; it is bitter, it takes too much to get drunk. My mid-teen booze of choice is to be found in the city's scrumpy pubs, drinking 'rough' cider with older hands at the homeless thing. The Wimpy Bar is closed on Christmas Day, so I wander around Plymouth Hoe. It is raining. My schooling is over. My future is uncertain. I am feeling sorry for myself. I look in on families, tinselled trees and fairy lights: Christmas card scenes. Exiled from nuclear normality, the Christmases I thought would be mine, I mourn my life, post care, post Peter Drabble. I return to the pub, to the other unloved. Later, someone takes me home for chicken dinner with his mother. A small kindness I can cling to.

DECEMBER 27. Denmark. The whooper swans arrive with the snow. Their calls haunt the bay, out of the cold, out of the mist, the swansong end of the day. Geese fly by in ragged ribbons and regimented Vs, like a wildfowl flight path. Ducks in their thousands cluster in the icy water. Winter is here. Cold as charity. Snow sticks to trees, our jackets and hats. We walk with the neighbours, sledging slopes with small kids, throw snowballs soft as marshmallow. We watch the suicidal kite surfers slice across the waves. Hailstorms tear at our windows. Ice gathers in neat piles like fish eggs or pearls. The day starts with a fire, the burble of burning logs and a Christmas candle. Up early as always, waiting for light and warmth, both in short supply. I scatter the bushes with bird-balls and wallow in the frenzied feeding. Here are canary-coloured yellowhammers, siskins, hawfinches. I have taken to watching them with binoculars, shouting at marauding crows when they try to steal the small birds' food. A hawk swoops, the hedge falls silent. A scarlet-chested bullfinch puffs in the cold. We are here for

Christmas and New Year to walk the wild beaches and clear the garden. Two-metre brambles are choking the bank. Fallen oak leaves are filling the ditch. There are old trees to cut down, new trees that need more light, young birch to straighten after being bent by winter gales. We buy new gardening gloves and get to work with rip saws and an axe: the tools of winter. We cut and clear. I tear out bramble by the roots until my arms cramp. We stop for a few days to enjoy the snow, squeaking as we walk. I read the runes of the tracks on the plot. Is it a cat, a pine marten, a fox or all three? The deer are easy. I read by firelight. I sleep easy and long. I cut tree trunks and stack them for next winter's wood. I rake smothering leaves to unearth the woodland plants. They may flower soon. Celandine is showing, a few confused daisies are out, even the lavender has bud. The small trees and I stand straighter when we leave.

DECEMBER 30. Christopher's birthday. I am worried my memory of him is fading. His voice thins and calls more quietly. I am caught between relief and mourning its missing. He has been insistent in my unconscious in the past year as the idea takes hold that he is gone. He is no longer to be searched for and found. We are beyond repair. Today, though, his voice is subdued. Has therapy shut him up or shut him out? December 30 was never a good birthday. Too close to Christmas, Dad said. Mine, too, only two weeks away. Chris's gift, maybe a pair of Tuff school shoes with a guarantee to stand wear and tear or your money back. Christopher wore and tore, not one to sit still. He had the best smile. It came less easily later. Unless he had a ball at his feet or in his hand. Here he was fluent.

Care records. Plymouth. 23.1.59. Christopher left with father by Mrs Jenkins. Christopher does not attend school.

Care records. Plymouth. 5.2.59. Alan was being cared for by Mr Jenkins's housekeeper while his father was working. This arrangement was satisfactory until Mrs Jenkins, who is divorced, brought Christopher to be cared for by his father. The boys have become out of hand and Mrs F is no longer able to look after them. How long is the child likely to be in care? Indefinitely.

It seems we all needed Ray to be the rescuer, the Samaritan saving his adopted son. But Christopher was a weapon in a war of attrition. A six-year-old being returned to his dad whatever the official papers might say. Why, I wonder. His new sanctuary was short-lived. The care home called.

DECEMBER 31. Danish New Year's Eve. I have bought a big box of fireworks for maybe the first time ever. We gather with neighbours on the beach at midnight. The moon is almost full. It shimmers on the sea. Other groups are here with rockets, air bombs and booze. The celebrations are optimistic, defiant of the future and the freezing wind. It is happy, hopeful, noisy, not the introspection I am used to. Clusters of flashing colours and bonfires punctuate the bay. Wrapped warm, we laugh, we light fireworks, we drink champagne and whisky. We look forward to the year.

JANUARY

JANUARY 6. Epiphany at the plot. An envelope has arrived from Jane Scotter, biodynamic grower by the Black Hills, Hereford. Small, fierce, slightly scary, she is my inspiration and gardening reality check. Every time I think I have grown something beautiful – and yes it happens – I visit her farm stall, see her land and realise how much I have to learn. The envelope contains the Three Kings preparation consisting of *Aurum metallicum* (gold), frankincense and myrrh. This is my favourite biodynamic mix at perhaps my least favourite time. Dusk on January 6 is rarely the right weather for sitting outside for an hour, dressed in office clothes, stirring cold water in a bucket.

January 6 is also Howard's birthday, so there are other gifts for him: cake and a bottle of whisky. We take it in turns to stir with our hands. The water is a little warmed at first, the fragrance of church, of hope and sadness, lifting as it swirls. Howard cuts slices of Epiphany *galette des rois* and we take it in turns wearing the gold paper crown. It is a good way to start the gardening year. After an hour, the water is too chilled, and so are we, but there has been a connection with time, place and each other.

We spray the mix around the edges of the plot, taking care to include Mary's. I leave for the cinema smelling like a choirboy.

JANUARY 11. After days of stormy wind and rain, the sun is shining. It is almost warm. Time to get shallots in. I clear ground and lift a few of last year's chard plants, stripped to the stem by pigeons. Some of the onions need replanting. The roots are pushing them out of the earth like rockets trying to launch. I make dibbing holes with my thumb and bed them in. I settle on a space and lay a long hazel stick as a rule. I hoe a rill and space the shallots evenly. I mooch around and tidy, clearing weeds and chicory leaves. The mustard, too hot for pigeons perhaps, is budding and almost ready to flower. I pick a little, it tastes of heat and exotic travel. The few radishes left by the snails are woody but welcome. I take a small chicory for tea. I am joined by my neighbours. Ruth is scoping out beds for potatoes, keen, like me, to sow. John has brought loppers to prune the elder at the bottom of his plot. Ruth and I make plans to attack the trees shading her corner. Howard and I have to sort the path planks that need replacing. There is tidying work to do now the days are just (I think) a little lighter.

JANUARY 13. The paradox of presents. I have started tearing up again in therapy. It is a habit I want to break. I normally see it coming, swerve before impact like avoiding being hit by a car. But sometimes, some things and names, some feelings, cannot be contained. My reservoir is too full to hold them. The dam bursts. Tears spill. This time I am trying to understand why birthday (or other) presents disturb me. Why I delay opening them as long as possible. Longer than is polite. How can unwrapping a gift make me anxious? Why do I want to hide? It has nothing to do with disappointment (well, there was a green alpaca sweater with a llama pattern once). It's something to do with privacy, sudden discomfort in the company of people who care. Three single syllables you strain to hear but can't. A phrase made banal from overuse. Yet sometimes, of a quiet morning, before or after, say, a birthday breakfast, 'I love you' burns deep until it is unbearable, and the thought conjures foolish tears to my eyes.

JANUARY 16. Birthday's over. I only had to hide once when opening a present. A quick trip to the plot: the sun shines, the blackbird sings on the wing, the pigeons skulk sullenly in trees. Food is thin on the ground so they've stripped the kale. Skeletons litter the plot, stranded empty brassica spines like a windblown burial ground. My heart quiets as I connect. The next day I return with Howard. We set up a sanctuary, moving the strongest of the small plants into a stockade. We are circling the wagons against winter and birds. We loop hazel poles to huddle mustard, chicories, stunted chard and beets together like stranded ewes in snow. It is the dead of winter but the onions and shallots have set, the deep-planted garlic is pushing through. Snowdrops are budding, daffodils showing, there is hope for the cold snap coming.

Family lore – for which read Uncle Mike when he was still eager to be seen as the archivist – is that I went into Dr Barnardo's the day I was born. My birthday seems a good time to see if there is any truth in it. I have mixed feelings about Barnardo's, the before-and-after-care cards, the 'philanthropic abductions' that parents called kidnapping. I mourn the way they separated traumatised siblings by sex. It has closed its orphanages – a number are under investigation for abuse – and rebranded its past. I fill in the form, add the asked-for ID and drop it in the post. I started this search when I was 60, older than my mother and brother when they died, time near my end to unravel my beginning.

JANUARY 17. I carry three dried black beans in my gardening jacket pocket, Cherokee Trail of Tears left over from a summer sowing a couple of years ago. The fact there are three is important, though I am unsure why. My hand strays to them, my fingers seek them out, almost unconsciously searching until I feel all three and relax.

JANUARY 18. I have been gardening with Howard for nine years now. He stuck the course at allotment one and two. He knows the names of plants. I don't make male friends easily, women always less of an issue. I had a theory as a kid that boys are like trees with taproots – just a few deep friends – while girls' roots branch out – but maybe that was about me and moving around, my too many names and schools and homes. My friendship with Howard grew organically, if you will. We agree on most things, though his quiet disapproval aces my overenthusiasm. What Howard brings to the plot is discipline, a depth of knowledge and his daughters, Nancy and Rose. They were toddlers when we started, forever digging holes, dwarfed by three-metre corn and sunflowers, getting almost lost, like in a Rousseau jungle. Building a special place, semi-wild and grown from seed, where children can play is at the heart of what we do. If Nancy and Rose approve, we know we're not far wrong. Nancy is older, maybe more sensitive, an inspired arranger of flowers; Rose is fiercer, more instinctive. They both took immediately to biodynamics, eager to stir, whatever the mix, excited to spray and share. For the hour before their patience wears thin and they want their dad to leave, they are the perfect companions on Plot 29, with a keen-eyed appreciation for flavours and colours. The allotment wouldn't be what it is without them.

JANUARY 19. I find myself anxious about the Barnardo's form. As a journalist, I have learned the five Ws – who, what, where, when, why. They are all needed to tell a story, we are taught, but too many are missing in my tale. I know the who. But when and where and why is harder to tell. I have lived with my lack of an early narrative, found strength in it, trusting my instincts. It has fashioned who and how I am. But it is not enough now. And I am not sure I understand why. Is it the Drabbles dying, my grandparents, my mother, my brother, each death cutting at my connection to the past? Each with chapters of their story untold. In Basildon, Ray sits sick, unable, he tells my sister, to talk to me. The past is too painful, he says – the story he has always stuck to. He is in his late eighties now. When he dies, his truths will be buried with him. For now, I am exhausting every other option, gathering clues like a private eye. My mother's family have closed the door, just Uncles Tony and Terry left. I have told them I am writing about Christopher and me. Colin isn't happy. No one remembers anything any more, so they say. Their gaudy sister bringing up bastard boys in the next room while they went to school; it is as though it never happened. The pride the family once took in me is clotting now. I was never much bothered before. I didn't feel a need to know. But Christopher whispers in my ear, asks me to remember, and a louder voice inside is increasingly insistent.

JANUARY 22. One month since the winter solstice, the temperature is averaging four or five degrees. There is night frost, it is cold, but the days are a little longer, the first signs of spring cannot be too far away. Seeds have arrived in the post. A care package from Mads McKeever at Brown Envelope in Ireland. Burgundy amaranth, Czech Black chilli, Amish Gold tomato, Lazy Housewife beans from Andalusia in Spain. Even the names are evocative. A colourful garden stirs. I plunder the catalogues and scour the seed sites. In truth, it is time to sort through the boxes, bags and drawers of seed to see what we are missing, what is too old, but that is so much less sexy. It is like turning the pages of a holiday brochure longing for blue seas and exotic cities. I order broad beans, snow peas, multiple packs of seasonal salad. Summer will be delivered in the post. I press send.

> Care records, Plymouth. 23.1.59. Tonsils and adenoids out last month. Quite fit for admission. Christopher good for admission, please can he be seen by a dentist fairly soon. Christopher had a hernia operation when about three. To see specialist in Feb. Boys out of hand. Christopher left with father by Mrs Jenkins. Christopher not at school.

Christopher truly suffered from carsickness as a kid. Forever bent over ditches, into hedges, grass verges, retching while I stood helpless beside him, upwind, trying not to gag. The sour stink of fear and vomit flavoured our family trips. A care worker report of the ride to meet the Drabbles (we weren't to know we were being auditioned) talks of little else. Medication didn't much help. He huddled in the back. Driving was dangerous. Maybe he worried about where he was being taken, whether he would return. He may have had reason. Being moved about made him fearful. Did my mother farm him out like she did Caron? Was he in the way? Why was he so scared and small, why were his teeth so bad? Why a hernia operation aged 'about three'. I pore over the possibilities now. I rewind the past to protect him. Back-to-the-future parenting. Dudley loathed the sickness. He hated weakness. He wasn't good with it. But he loved cars. There was a new model every other year, always cash. The cloying smell of new upholstery polluted by Chris's fear. He gradually grew out of it, I think, as the bad memories faded and he learned to trust and feel at home. He would later make a living from driving. I have only once been behind a wheel.

JANUARY 24. Biodynamic gardening comes with theories and philosophies that we don't much follow. It also comes with a lunar planting calendar we stick to. It maybe shouldn't work but it does. I blame Jane Scotter. If her produce didn't look happier, last longer, I wouldn't be struggling to find time to sow beetroot seed at 5am on a summer Saturday morning or hand stirring cow manure in a water bucket in the rain. Biodynamics can be inconvenient. We didn't just jump into it, we visited Jane's farm, Fern Verrow. There was no denying it there. It's a kid's colouring book come to life: a fairy-tale farm, with bees, sheep, cows and field after field of extraordinary crops, well husbanded and healthy. It was from these first visits that I learned to let some things live a fuller life through to flower and seed, to 'listen' to the land.

JANUARY 26. Another night of the hunted, another murder dream where I call hopelessly for help. My voice is thin, almost inaudible, no one can hear me or, if they do, they quickly look away. I finally get up at 4.30am. It is a relief to be awake, to make tea to take away the metallic taste and try to make sense of the recurring dread. Barnardo's has replied. They are 'pleased to confirm that we have identified you in our records'. I wish they weren't so pleased. They have a waiting list of 'approximately 14 months', so are 'giving priority to people aged 80 or older, those suffering critical illness or disability, and people who have suffered abuse in child-hood' – a hierarchy of hurt, the worthy unworthy, the dying and the damned.

Sometime next year I will be invited to see the documents. Before the Data Protection Act, they were excluded from legislation entitling people to see their files. Meanwhile, I scope the internet for images of baby dormitories, addresses of Dr Barnardo's Homes in Plymouth, stories of survivors. It is not a peaceful way to start a day.

Anxiety deepens during the next therapy session. How old am I in the dreams, she asks. Why is my voice so small? Do they always hunt in packs? Are they always only men? She probes gently. All I can say with certainty is that my helplessness has coagulated into 40 years or more of a recurring dream: of being hunted and hurt, caught up close. It's intimate, with blood. Back in the room of the tissues and tears, the childish pictures on the walls, the acting-out sandbox with traces of a child's fingers, my chest burns. My voice breaks. I am anxious to avoid the cliff. I have a meeting at work in 30 minutes. They are expecting a dynamic editor, not a broken man, red eyed. Somehow I had been hoping Dr Barnardo's wasn't true, that I hadn't joined the babies in their prison rows of iron cots. He was clever, Thomas Barnardo, a master of conjuring cash with a faked-up photo studio set up to look like a grubby street. Kids' clothes not raggedy enough would be rent with knives. The Dr Barnardo's Home collection box was shaped like a country cottage. This was a man with a refined understanding of the iconography of need. His appeal was based on a fresh start, wiping away the past. But what if he or she is a baby just days or weeks old? What if they want their mum? What then about the memories? The switch from therapy room to office desk, raging baby to adult, is tough today. It doesn't help that it's winter. In summer I would head to the plot, potter around at dawn, mooch about at dusk, pick a few weeds, a few leaves, a few flowers; a secret garden for my secret fears. It is unsettling, the not knowing, but the knowing is too. When my uncle told me I was there, it was just another chapter in my colourful tale, another note in my scrapbook. I don't have all the dates yet but it must have been bleak to be that baby.

JANUARY 27. It is four years today since Christopher died. Sometimes I feel my memories of him also slipping away. Perhaps this journal is an attempt to fix him before he (and I) fade too far. The images I have of him are becoming younger. I don't see the cancer-haunted, hollow man so strongly any more, I see the strutting soldier boy with mirror-polished shoes, the hazel-eyed, freckled country kid, grinning and leaning on his cricket bat in the sun-dappled croft. He would batter the balls I threw to him, we would laugh as I ran to retrieve them. He was happy then, with his new kitten, his new friends, and I want to wrap him in that perfect moment before it started again to unravel. I had thought when I started this book that it would be mostly about Dudley, flowers, fruit and vegetables, and me. A thank you for family, where I learned to grow. At its heart, though, it is a candle I light for Christopher, my big brother who was too small for too long, whose flame flickered. I can't bear the thought I wasn't there for his cremation. A cruel cut-off. Her words: we burnt him, burn through me. But I was there when he found his voice, when he laughed, when he learned what he was good at, when he was so close to being OK.

JANUARY 31. The day starts with snow. Swooning, slow flakes, rare in the city. Ruth has asked for help, the big pond has been overflowing, flooding her plot. There is promise of soup. It is sleeting. There is much cutting and chopping, trimming of trees. I work with buckets. The half-thought plan is to part-empty the pond and see if we can spot a leak in the lining. One leg in the fetid water, one leg out, I fill and fetch. It is slow, heavy work but I am joined by a young boy who wants to take over. Soon we have a system: he scoops, I fill, his mum and others carry away. It works. The sleet is heavier now. I lend him my gloves. He grins. Men stand around discussing plans while women work. We resolve to replace the lining, making ever more extravagant guesses at the size of sheet we will need. We uncover a batch of fat frogs nestled into lining folds. It feels like a signal to stop. The site has been cleared, the weeds, reeds and cut-up branches wheelbarrowed away. The soup and sausages are hot. We huddle under leafless trees as the sleet sheets down and talk about spring planting plans and lemongrass. It feels like community, a gardening family. We drift away to our homes and Saturdays.

So, her hands scuffled
over the bakeboard,
the reddening stove ...
the scone rising
to the tick of two clocks.
And here is love

Seamus Heaney, 'Sunlight'

FEBRUARY

FEBRUARY 1. A cold, wet Sunday walk over Hampstead Heath. I am hooded and gloved, the mud sucking on my boots. First, as always, straight up the middle of Parliament Hill, stopping briefly to look out over the City, to see the Shard and spot St Paul's. Past the kite-flying dads looking to impress uninterested kids, through the gap and the clump of beeches, the first fallen tree. Past the family posing in the branches, a small girl laughing if she can stamp in a puddle. In summer I stop at the water fountain. I always linger on the viaduct. Sometimes I head north here to the allotment site; other times we turn right for a secluded spot where we buried the cats, wrapped in Kashmiri scarves that were later seen shredded by a fox. Today it is tea and cake at Kenwood. Past our picnic spot, the murder of black crows, the shrieking parakeets, down by the reeded lakes where there may or may not be a heron. We turn by the tennis courts, the lido and running track. Last, back over the bridge and home.

FEBRUARY 2. I am sitting at my desk, feeling disturbed. This is an open-plan newspaper office, with close seating like a call centre. I have been in a side room for a personal call to Barnardo's 'Making Connections' team. I want to make my case for reducing the waiting time to see my records. Fourteen months seems a lifetime away. I am not 80, I don't have a serious illness, so I need to know how they quantify abuse. Do I need proof and if so what kind? I have been practising. A helpful voice answers; I tell her my names: I am Allan Jenkins enquiring about the records for Alan Beale. With maybe one L and an E. I tell her I believe I was in Barnardo's as a baby. Yes, she says, too quickly, you came in at two months old. You are here in the computer. The air around me stills. I believe I stayed about a year, I say, treading delicately now. Baby steps. Yes, she says, before you were restored to your mother. 'Restored', I can't help thinking, a strange use of word, more common for a faded painting or a rundown cottage. Something needing work. I ask about the early-access rules, what criteria they use for 'abused as a child'. She says she believes it has to have been in Barnardo's. She puts me through to a social worker for clarity. The phone rings empty. My heart hits loud. She will have them call me tomorrow, she says.

I step out of the room, my legs light, my head unheld. I wasn't ready. I have no defence against this stuff. Two months. In caged beds. I don't know whether it is better than being a day old. I have *Observer* work to do, magazine pages to pass, stuff waiting for my approval. I read proofs, change some things, while her words turn around in my head. Like an unfamiliar taste, too salty, too strong. Luckily it is late, in an hour and a half I am home. I wasn't newborn in my Dr Barnardo's Home. I had (maybe) been with my mother. Long enough to bond, to need, to become familiar – with her smell, her feel, her taste, to be breastfed or bottled, who knows? Likely no one now. Long enough to know the missing. And why at two months? What had changed? Was I inconvenient?

FEBRUARY 3. I wake to snow on the roof terrace, plant and leaf outlines are softened. Old people struggle in the street, walking tentatively with sticks. I'm not liking this, says one to no one in particular. As I walk to the therapist, I too am more careful now, more aware of falls and hurt. Committed to excavating my story, unearthing my brother, I left it late. Unable to confront my mother, not ready to doorstep Ray, I rely on secondary sources: scraps, memories, clues from my uncles, records written never to be read. Too late to stop, like an old man out on the ice afraid of breaking something.

As I shuffle through Kentish Town I remember the carefree snow of '63, trudging to Aveton Gifford school, my last year there with Christopher before he bussed into Kingsbridge, two boys on the long walk, snow soft as Tunnock teacakes. There was a coal stove in the classroom surrounded by a cage. Dudley bought chains for his tyres and drove us to Dartmoor to marvel at the moonscape. I loved to run into the snowdrifts, arms outstretched, making me-shaped holes. A magical flamingo appeared on the river for a few days among the white, an exotic, incongruous pink. Denmark has that feeling for snow. It falls, it stays. I have another room with a stove to warm. Here, too, it lasts like Narnia, sculpted by the wind. I wrap up, I walk, I feel at home. I watch the swans appear out of the mist.

FEBRUARY 7. Most of my arguments happen in cars, confined, claustrophobic, catastrophic. Nought to 100 in short seconds. No way back. It took a psychoanalyst to point it out. I guess that's what I paid for, the search for patterns. Was it the old uncertainty, he asked, the child not knowing where he was going, what would happen, would he return? Did cars signal uncertainty, that you were no longer safe (was that why Christopher was sick)? Awareness cooled it for a while. But it is back now as I peel away my carefully crafted life, the Allan Jenkins onion, the pass-the parcel kid. Uncovering my avatars like a Russian doll. I am driven now by a need to know. To know more at least, though it sometimes spills into molten fury, barely capped. This is what the therapy is for, to avoid Pompeii. I used to see myself as an occasional melancholic. Calmed by the cello, songs of loss, whisky, food, walking, and gardening of course. I didn't acknowledge anger. Maybe because it wasn't allowed as a care kid. It didn't fit with the lovability formula: the ever eager over-gratitude. Now I try to spot the tsunami alert, be more aware of seismic shifts before it explodes in the confines of a car.

1964. Food isn't a thing for Mum and Dad. It is almost always fresh, there is always enough but it is for fuel, not pleasure. There are no people dropping by to feed. There is no fish for somewhere so close to the coast, except the occasional herring for tea, fried in oatmeal with its roe, my favourite thing; an occasional plaice for Dad's ulcer, steamed on a plate with milk. There are home-grown runner beans, peas and potatoes. There is cake, ginger or parkin (fruit cakes are for Christmas), but best is Victoria sponge. Dusted with sugar, two halves with homemade strawberry jam, a smaller slice for us. There are rice puddings, plum pies. Peaches are tinned, so are pears, though we have a number of trees in the croft. Our tastes are muted and polite.

Shrimps are my undoing, my Damascene me-moment. It is the Sunday School trip, a day on Paignton beach. I am aged maybe 10. The sun shines. The sand is inviting. The sea is warm. I never leave the seafood stall. I have half a crown to spend. I mean to buy an ice cream, perhaps a 99. I have never eaten shrimps but the smell is enticing. There are winkles, cockles, the sharp hit of vinegar. I've never had vinegar, never had chips, I have never had shrimps. I buy a small cone for sixpence. I peel each shrimp slowly. Undress it. Put it in my mouth. Sun and sand and sea. This is better than a Wall's wafer. I order another cone, and another after that. I am hooked. It is kiddie heroin. There is a briny sweetness to them, salt explosions going off in my mouth. Some I can't be bothered to peel, I like the crisp crunch and the coral eggs. My brother and the other kids are building castles decked with paper flags. Light dances on the waves. I buy five cones one after another, though I try to slow down, like saving the ending of a favourite book. And then it is over. My money has run out. I don't remember being on the beach but I remember this moment. The taste of the sea, eaten by the sea, a sensual world away from Aveton

Gifford. I don't know it at the time, just that these flavours are mine. They tell me something of who I am and where I come from. The next summer trip it rains, so we go to Kent's Cavern and eat ice cream on the coach. I still buy a small scoop of brown shrimps most weeks from an old-school stall at the farmers' market. Now I dress them with a squeeze of lemon, a scant hit of Aleppo chilli. Sometimes Sunday school doesn't seem so far away.

The river runs through me. The Devon Avon not 100 feet from my bedroom window, at the front of Herons Reach. It separates us from the village. Sometimes close by, sometimes far away. Twice a day with the tide, I watch the Stakes Road disappear, the river come to cut us off, transform our little world. Dad tells us the man who had the house before us was a farmworker, found drowned in the mud. He came home drunk one night, he said, fell face down. The more he sought to escape, the more he was stuck. I never knew if it was true but Dad wasn't one for stories.

Our twin paths to school are different, like the choices we will make. One is short and flat, perhaps seaweedy; wet and a little wild. The other, if the tide is high, is up a long, hilly lane by houses, high hedges, rooted in land. Christopher always prefers to turn towards the farm, his friends, the reassuring company of boys. I am drawn to the bank. The river means freedom, a place of possibilities. Curlews call me like the pied piper. For Chris, though, it means fishing. There are muddy grey mullet, impossible to catch, impossible to eat. Fishing isn't about food for Chris. He hunts with his friends for rabbits. He shoots crows, pigeons, hares – the hardest to forgive. Genocide kids. I hate the hunters. There are otter hounds on the river, harriers in the fields, fox hunters everywhere. Worst is badger baiting, breaking the wild animal's legs before sending the terriers in. Harmless village sport for boys letting off steam, but not for me. So I turn left out of the gate in search of magic and mystery. My tidal place of death-dealing mud, mist and unpredictable change.

There are hares at the summerhouse. The next road is named after them. They lope through the garden if we are lucky, a flash of orange, brown and legs. Sometimes one will be sitting there when we arrive and turn unhurried away. We often see them on the path, an almost lazy movement like a loosely articulated dream. They seem wilder somehow than rabbits, more solitary, mysterious. Sometimes I spot one lying low in the field, ears flat. One shares the sunset with us once. Out of the trees on to the beach. Sitting bolt upright, facing west, the sun and sea. It sits still for a long time till the sun drops and the sky turns. Suddenly, explosively, it speeds effortless, along the long beach, wild and exhilarating.

13.2.62. The school teacher had spoken to Mr Drabble who at the beginning had compared one boy with the other, pointing out how unfair this would be.

There was the time with the watch. Christopher is given a Timex when he goes to secondary school. It is small, cheap, a little childish for his age, but he loves it and lords it over me. I will have to wait another year until I, too, am 11. It was a Dudley rule. Reward, I guess, not a random gift, not the Drabble way. So in 1965 when I pass the 11-plus I am handed one too. Except mine is bigger, shinier, almost adult. I am ashamed to say I am proud, though smug might be more accurate.

Sometimes I fear that for Dad we were a mixed pair, buy one, get one free. I often felt he was harsher with Christopher, less patient than with me. There is a thread through the records, a constant drip of disappointment: when Christopher didn't excel in school, when he was less eager to endlessly please. When he kept his name, though Dad shamefully didn't insist. Perhaps Christopher had a stronger sense of who he was. He harboured hurt for longer. He couldn't help it. His world was painted black and white. I dealt less in certainty. In the Plymouth records Dudley writes repeatedly of handing him back and holding on to me. He is looking to cut their losses. Christopher must have known. He must have felt it. They pushed him into the army when I went to private school. In the end it switched. When I turned troublesome, they kept with Chris. There is an admiring note about his shooting five hares one morning. Maybe they just didn't have the energy or appetite for both boys. I wish they had found out earlier. Christopher might have felt more wanted. We might still have been together. I cling to him like seaweed now that there are just shards of him left.

1968. Mum is confused by vegetarians. There must be meat on a plate. A life of Edam looms in front of me – cheese and two veg. She cannot understand not wanting gravy. A few bones can't make much difference. A half-moon slice of bland cheese, boiled potatoes, most likely cabbage, day after day. The Edam is there for Dad's cream crackers after we have gone to bed. I am always trying tastes I can't find at home. They rarely work well. The tin of 'meatless goulash' is a disappointment, poorly matched for lunch with Mum's pudding rice. I lurk around the health-food shop on Kingsbridge quay. It is packed with tins and foreign voices and flavours. My friends all talk about yogurt so I start with that. It is essentially milk that has turned in the sun. Later I find out that the yogurt other kids like is Ski: pink or purple with jam. Raw sheep's milk isn't yet a thing. I have been reading about olives, too: spies and other sophisticates have them in martinis, perhaps in Monte Carlo, playing chemin de fer (Mum and Dad don't hold with cards, so we avoid local whist drives as though they are white-slave dens of vice). I buy a jar of olives on my way home from school. This can't be right, I tell myself: unspeakably briny and bitter. Disappointed, I dump them in a bin. My feeble rites of passage reach their peak with whisky. I retch. This cannot be it? It will be 20 years until I try again. Too much reading and not enough living is taking a toll. Sex is the same, and cigarettes. I stubbornly persist with these.

FEBRUARY 14. My breathing is shallow. I want to comfort. I want to be comforted. It is Valentine's Day and I have spent the afternoon with three of my sisters. Mandy lives in South Carolina. She and Lesley have met only twice. We are all meeting with Susan, who is also in therapy. Over lunch and later at a bar, Susan and Mandy's stories of living with my mother spill out. Of being young and vulnerable in her home. Of rape and predator parties. The prostitute working from the front room.

Lesley thinks she is a hermit. She fears she is unlovable. She doesn't remember me showing her photos of Sheila. The memory has burrowed down into the place where the crusts are kept. Loved-up couples come into the bar for Valentine's Day drinks. I walk my sisters back to the station and take Susan's arm. As we cross the road to Charing Cross, her hand reaches out for mine. I squeeze it. The shattered childhood we never shared. All the while, my wife Henri is in our kitchen making marmalade. The house smells of home and oranges. The scent of Lilian. I want to hide.

FEBRUARY 15, MORNING. A night of shallow sleep, of lying awake. It is before 5am when I get up. I drink tea and start with marmalade. Mum made two jams: strawberry in summer, from fruit we grew. It was the only jam Dad would eat. At South Milton, he swapped a piece of land for another plot for strawberries. She made marmalade in winter. I remember coming home from primary school. I was small. It was raining. The kitchen was alive with exotic steam. I had never had marmalade and now I had a mum in a kitchen preparing something serious. It smelled exotic and it smelled of family. It is the only jam I eat. At boarding school we had it with sausages and bacon, my first 'foodie' experience. Now there are jars lined up waiting to be filled. There is a large pan covered with a chequered cloth, steeping overnight. Love is sleeping upstairs.

February

FEBRUARY 15, NOON. It is the second instalment of the pond working party and I am relieved to have something physical to do. We bucket out the last of the muddy water, rehoming the confused frogs. We uncover a baby newt, curled up, golden eyed and half asleep. We re-line the pond. The mains water is turned off for winter so we refill it with buckets from butts and tanks scattered around the site. We ferry and fetch. We admire our efforts. We stop with the water about two-thirds full. The forecast is for rain. There will be another work party in a couple of weeks when we will replant flowers around the edges and trim more trees, but for now there's hot carrot soup and spicy sausages. We sit in the nearly warming sun and talk about *Wolf Hall*. It is very Hampstead. I am happy. Howard and I will be back in a week to clear the plot and sow broad beans. We will debate whether to grow potatoes. The gardening year starts here.

> 16.2.59. The boys are settled into their new life, and appear to be agile little fellows. Christopher is very small considering he is the eldest of the two. Both are proud of their being brothers.

2005. It is Lilian's funeral, in Bedford near her niece. She had spent her last year here, in sheltered housing, after being conned out of £3,000. They had come to clean her gutters, they said, then driven her to the bank where she drew out cash for a new patio and, of course, they never came back. She was 95, she had a good life, a good marriage, a good death. She had been loved and now it is over. We were better together in the five years after Dad died. More at peace. I used to pop down to Devon to see her, trying not to show concern while she shakily poured me tea. For her I would be Peter again, tell her my news while she'd serve the cake she still made. After the funeral service, her niece asks about 'your half brother'. It hits me. Everyone had known, just not Christopher and I. The first of my mother's seven children by seven fathers (almost sounds like a film). We clung to each other as long as we could. Now I am the eldest of six survivors who share some of the same blood, much of the same pain. You can sometimes see on their faces that something bad has happened.

FEBRUARY 17. There is a small handprint in the therapist's sand. Another child hurt, too young to know the words to describe it. Too small to talk about the betrayal, the feelings so big they stick. Some silences are screams that haven't yet found their voice. I have heard them. I cry, of course, in the room today. There is no smart way to avoid the hopelessness of not being able to protect my brothers and sisters. I reach for a tissue, spill the terrible secrets and tears. Some things are buried under an amnesia blanket. Maybe medicated away. Susan and Lesley's lives in some ways mirror each other, like an experiment with separated twins. They are on the same anti-depressants. They both have large memory gaps. Susan says she doesn't remember much before she was 12. Mine start at five, Lesley's much later. Sometimes memories stir like crocodiles. Sometimes in the right company or with the right professional, they can be exposed.

I waited for Sheila for more than 30 years. I had hoped that if only I met my mother everything would heal. I never had a yen for a father. It was my mother who would hold me. I imagined she would be wild with big breasts, big hair. She wouldn't hold back like Lilian. She would be the opposite of Ray. There would be no secrets. We would share stories. We would talk. We would hold hands. We would cook, sit in the kitchen, laughing. We could be friends. It was, of course, childish fantasy but nearly true for a few days. The phone call from Susan and the one when my mother and I first talked. Her voice and tone close to mine. It was there on the train to Portsmouth. The hope I would be folded into my mother's understanding arms. I knew it was dangerous, my Hollywood dream, all my eggs in her basket. Cue soft colours, roll credits. It lasted up to the front door but it couldn't survive her standing there. Be careful what you wish for. She is in my blood, a sluggish slowness, a hateful hating rage. She is my virus to be inoculated against so it doesn't pass to my children's children.

FEBRUARY 20. I have been heart-sick all week. Feelings trapped like indigestion, as if everything would be all right if only I reached for an antacid. It is hard to swallow my sisters' history. Some truths, once seen, are seared. Was Ray right all those years ago? Was it better never to know? I need to break the spell. There is a plant fair today at London's Horticultural Halls. The streets are packed with people. Hellebore, hepatica, snowdrops bursting out of bags. The halls are fragrant with early flowers from specialist nurseries dealing in spring. Here are primroses, wood anemone and iris. I soak it in as if I had woodland and acres of meadow to plant. I stop by the violet stand, remember the posies I picked from hedgerows in the days when it was still OK. I buy two pots as though they are for Lilian: one deeply coloured, the other *Viola odorata*, smelling of old ladies and sweets. I watch kids potato-printing. On the tube back to work, I stick my head in the violet bag and breathe.

FEBRUARY 22. I place seed potatoes in an old egg tray to chit, keep them in a cool spot. It is only four weeks from the spring equinox; there is heavy work to do. The rehomed battered planting hasn't taken at the plot. The trauma was too tough, the soil too wet and unwelcoming. Sometimes I imagine I can hold back winter like Canute. I decide to clear the plot. I am digging a replanted chicory bed when I discover potatoes, lots of them. I'd left them there last summer when Howard was away; I wanted his family to have them. They have been in the soil ever since. There is a bucketful by the time I have dug the bed over. I bag them up and cover them. I can't take them with me into town.

FEBRUARY 23, SUNDAY. Back at the plot, I set to work. The forecast is for rain. The sun is out, though there is a frosted silver crust on the ground. Both ponds are iced over. I hope the newt has forgiven us the eviction to the smaller pond. The frogs will be spawning soon and it is going to get crowded. It is 10am and the site, as always, is empty. I clear the netting, lift the pegs and poles, grub up almost everything, though I am a little uncomfortable with only garlic and onions growing. I need small spots of colour to break up the brown. I turn the claggy soil. It is winter work with serious tools. By lunchtime, it is as though last year's plot hardly happened. The ground is ready for growing. I have saved a bright pink radish from the last autumn planting with Polly. I brush off the mud. It is crisp with a little heat. I pick a radicchio and put it in my pocket to add to a cheese sandwich for lunch. It is food fit for gods and gardeners.

FEBRUARY 26. I keep losing things or, more accurately, I think I do. I am going through a fretful phase, forever emptying out bags and drawers or pockets in a frantic search for stuff that isn't lost. Boarding passes, my passport, tickets, cash, memories – nothing is safe. I spill out the contents repeatedly. I guess what I have lost is me. I have always been strong or so I liked to think – comfortable in my own company – but memories are undoing me, like scraping away paint on a door, stripping comfort like layers of clothes until I feel smaller, colder, more naked and alone. Am I revealing a new (old?) fearful me? Is the voice I hear a child who's late for loving, a fearful man with early-onset dementia, or is it simply a response to picking at the scab of my life till it bleeds?

FEBRUARY 27. A late-night cinema changed my life and luck for ever. I was 27. I was with a friend who needed drink and company. It was almost midnight in Hampstead; Saturday-night movies in an art-house cinema with a bar. I was a little drunk when I saw her. Blonde hair, an amused smile in a mirror, ice-blue eyes that saw (through) me. She was with someone who was inattentive and I couldn't understand why. Our glances caught a couple of times. Then, too late, she was going in. Except he went first. I stepped in, stopped the door to talk to her, some feeble chat about vodka, whether she would carry in orange juice for us. We didn't want to drink it neat (those innocent days). She smiled and agreed, so I asked her to sit with us. We watched Kurosawa's *Kagemusha*. We kissed. She slid down the chair to hide from her friend. She moved in with me three weeks later, 33 years ago, sharing decades of happiness I never thought I'd have. It is her birthday tomorrow, February 28, the last day of winter. Sunday will be spring. I will sow seed and thank my lucky stars for Henri, my wife, for my life, for love.

8.6.60. Christopher is gradually losing his nervousness and does not talk so much now about when he lived in Portsmouth.

If Plymouth was purgatory, Portsmouth was hell. I am tormented by thoughts of what might have happened to Christopher with my mother and her men. He was seven now, his life misshapen, his twisted destiny too tough to escape, though he would fight until exhaustion and age and cancer tore him down. I cannot break away from something my sister Mandy said about hernias in three-year-olds being mostly caused by crying. I find comfort at first in the hope that perhaps he wasn't raped. Why don't I remember he came to me as a child from

Portsmouth? Why didn't he remember he had been with Sheila or her proxies all that time? She had stuck to her line that she'd had to run away with her baby. Was she never concerned the truth would out: that Christopher would remember, break the spell of forgetfulness she'd spun for all her children? I'd thought I must have made up my dark memories, embellished them, but there is a truth at their heart that holds to scrutiny, threadbare though they are. There are worse things than disease and being locked in cupboards. Increasingly it seems Lesley and I have survived by being kept from my mother.

MARCH

MARCH 1. Allotment, early. I am away later for a couple of days and it is the start of spring: time to sow the first seed. I can feel the shift. There is warmth in the air. I check for spawn. The new pond needs finishing and the irises replanting. The plot is looking bare, impatient; a teenage boy with a fresh trim for a first date. I hoe a bed at the southern end, make a dibber from a piece of hazel pole. The soil is still wet and cold, the earth slow to follow the sun. I have brought Brown Envelope Seeds broad beans – old-variety crimson-flowered, the most alluring bean I have seen. There was also calendula at the bottom of the tin. I check the secret spot for wild garlic and sure enough it is there – a shock of pungent green in the bank.

MARCH 4. Therapy. We are at the choking, broken heart of it now, the space of tears a rushing torrent taking all before it. There is nothing I can do. There was nothing then. I was too small to save my sisters. I wasn't there. We had never met. I think about this room and how many here have cried. The tiny handprints in the sandbox, today a little finger pattern like leopard spots. I get my coat and carry on. There is a magazine to get out and family to love.

MARCH 7, SATURDAY. Spring. The weekend sun is already stronger. Today is close to 15°C. The plot is calling. It's really too early to sow too much but it's time to sort seed. I root around the house, collecting packets from bags and boxes and tins. I lay them out on the floor, grouped into herbs and salads, root vegetables, fruits, flowers, kales and chards. This may come in useful later. Some I should maybe throw away but I'll give them a chance, like someone once gave me (and yes, I know how that sounds). On site, the unfinished pond is teeming with frogs. The males are noisy, overactive, the females overwhelmed. I trudge a few more buckets of water to the pond. I sit in the sun, watching bees, even butterflies. The hives are alive. I sow more garlic. I lay in a row of radishes. You never know.

Sometimes when I think of this book, I am almost bewildered it has taken such a turn. It was to be about gardening, a year in the life of a piece of land, with personal stuff added in. The tone has taken me by surprise. It is lacking in laughter, the growing the only light to balance shade. When I read it back, my voice softens, becomes smaller. Writing it is like dropping down a mine. I head out to the seam and see what's to be found. It's not properly planned like my other work, with quotes, a beginning, a middle, an end. It's more like my gardening. I have to listen before I have something to say.

MARCH 9, SUNDAY. We are measuring the boardwalk at the bottom of the plot. Mary has put her foot through a plank. Back from Istanbul, she is here today with more feed for her birds. Her bag is bursting with plants. A vivid green angelica sticks out of the top. Our neighbour Jeffrey is digging David's plot. It is overgrown and the committee has warned they will take it off him if it isn't fixed. David is a retired Africa hand for the *Financial Times*. He visits his plot most days, eats a banana, throws its skin in his compost bin. He isn't up to digging. His wife has asked Jeffrey for help. Howard and I give him a hand. We slice the grassy top layer off, careful not to disturb the asparagus, the one bold leek standing proud. It is like cutting turf, tiring. We clear a bed, fill a couple of wheelbarrows with weed, before Howard has to leave. Rose needs help with her homework.

12.3.59. Alan is very excitable and chatters constantly, both are looking well except Christopher is so small.

1970. Fried rice is one of my first discoveries that show how I am different from Dudley. There are other strands in my DNA. I am 16, living on carbon tetrachloride and cartons of takeaway rice. It is Chinese, cheaper than chips. A box of something exotic, bland and comforting. There are greasy pictures on the wall: softly shaped islands and boats with Asian sails. I never venture far from the rice. I don't have the same feeling for sweet and sour, though the pineapple has an appeal like my first curry with raisins in boarding school. I have a thing for

Kentucky fried chicken for a short while, the crisp crust concealing the sweet meat inside. I try it again when I come to London. It is somehow slimy, tasting of fear and fish.

MARCH 13. There is a message from Barnardo's. The tone has changed, my records should be ready in a couple of weeks. I can come in or receive them by post. The choice is mine, the mail says.

14.3.59. Impetigo, scabies, herpes simplex.

I crave hugs. I long to be held. I have felt incomplete without it much of my life. I can do cuddles and massage. I have worked on this. But don't come quietly up behind me. Never stroke my neck. It is instant, the reaction, like a trip wire or the emergency cord on a train. Just a loving brush near the back of my head and I am flooded with fear. I go into lockdown. My emergency shutters crash. I can't connect to the kindness or any loving intent. All I get is a body memory that my brain no longer holds. Something bad happened. My mind is amnesiac but my body less so.

MARCH 15. On the Danish coast. I am caught in heavy rain cycling the coastal road in Denmark. I have a puncture. I am soaked to the skin. Too far from home, I make it to my mother-in-law's. I put my clothes in her dryer. I sit in my underpants, my modesty covered by a desk. We drink tea, we wait for the rain to stop and my jeans and woollen jacket to dry. An hour or two later, on my way to the summerhouse, I am happy, my tyre repaired. My hand snakes to my pocket, fingers search for three beans that are no longer there ...

MARCH 16. Waves lap at the shore, I pick white seashells, gather them in my pocket. The beach is still. Me too, rare in these days of digging deep. I feel worries wash away, comforting memories wrap round me, soft like angora. The rhythmical song of the water reorders my anxieties. You belong here, it says, like Lilian once said. This is your home. The hare's here too. I am not sure why it matters so much – seeing it wander through the plot. I watch as it takes its time, scratches at the grass, sits up, all ears, super alert, moves fluidly through the space. Stop, look, listen, unhurry away. Spring is always a month later here, snowdrops are spreading, wood anemones streaming out into the grass, but it's the hepatica that catches the moment, flashes a subdued violet among the dead leaves in the hedgerow. It is easy to miss. I lie in the ditch to admire the nodding flower as yet unready. The firewood has arrived. Beech and oak, Denmark and England, slow-burning, heat-giving hardwood. Five cubic metres is a small mountain. We are lucky with the weather, bright sun but not too warm. The neighbours arrive with a wheelbarrow, my brother-in-law and mother-in-law are here. We set up a system: some stacking, some freighting. Others sorting by size. The shed fills with patterns of logs and light. There is new space for another blackbird nest, another hazelnut hiding place: the red squirrel stash. In three hours or so, it is done. We stop, we drink Easter beer or tea, or both. We light a bonfire in a barrel, like the one Mum used to incinerate my jeans. We burn the cleared bramble. I break up small branches and feed them in. White smoke and the day drifts easy. The woodpile is gone. The shed is packed. The bonfire space is cleared. The summerhouse plot is ready for spring. The outdoor housekeeping's done. Before we leave, we plant violets in the bank and pot up lily of the valley for later in the year. I have been sleeping nine or 10 hours a night, twice the rest I get in London.

MARCH 18, WEDNESDAY MORNING. I am in Barnardo's in east London reading my records – the familiar language, the familiar tone, the familiar players: I am being put up for adoption, the notes say. Sheila is 19, pregnant for the third time. She had a miscarriage at 17. Christopher at 18. I will be next. Billy and Doris have had enough so they have brought her here. Sheila is described as '*medium build, mid-brown hair, brown eyes – dull and suppressed in presence of M.Gd-fa [maternal grandfather: Billy] who was curt with her*'. She's been seen by Dr Matheson of the mental health department who '*did not consider her certifiable as a feeble-minded person*', though my great-aunt, Marina Beale, '*is in the care of the Royal Western Counties Mental Institution*'. Poor woman, whoever she was.

The records state that my grandparents are respectable people and their home is overcrowded. Four of my uncles live in one room, aged 11 to 17. Christopher is there too, in a cot. It says they are devoted to him. My mother will not be allowed to bring me back from the maternity home. Something must be done quickly, my grandmother says. Sheila's 'character' and 'morals' are reported to be 'weak'. I feel like an intruder. We are here at last, before the beginning. The start of my life in single-spaced type.

12.02.1954. Four weeks old:

Dr Barnardo's Homes: National Incorporated Association.
Head Offices – 1–26, Stepney Causeway London, E1

[Sixpence stamp]

I Sheila Irene Beale
of 57, Grassendale Avenue, Swilly, Plymouth
being the mother of Allan Peter Beale
hereby agree with the Association:

to the child entering into the care of Dr. Barnardo's Homes and to the child being brought up by the Association in any of its branches, or in any of its boarding-out homes in the British Isles:
    to the child being brought up in the Protestant Faith:
    to the Association, without further consultation, taking such action in respect of the child as may be deemed necessary in the child's interest:
    to the Association placing the child when it deems it proper in that occupation which it considers best for the child.

To abide by the rules of the Association, and to co-operate with its officers in their efforts on the child's behalf:

to receive back the child in my care if at any time requested to do so.

Dated this Friday 12th day of February 1954

Signature and address SI Beale
57 Grassendale Ave
Swilly

Signatures and addresses of two witnesses
[redacted]

Four weeks old and the right to choose my occupation is on the list? I break it all down into bite-sized pieces: the photo of my Barnardo's Home with prams outside, the details of my mother's room. Ray is on the scene now, they are going to be married. He will take my brother but I am too much to ask. My grandmother describes me as a '*handsome baby – much nicer than Christopher when he was born*'. The comparisons begin. There is another note from Billy pleading for speed but Barnardo's still doesn't have space. It may take three months. Time enough to be breastfed, time enough to bond. The notes ask what I will be weaned on when the escort comes to take me. But bigger news waits innocent as a kitten, unexploded ordinance in eight-point type.

There is a name where it asks for father: FRANCIS O'TOOLE, AGED 22, LEADING COOK ON HMS *DECOY*. Of course, I have never heard of him, it isn't the name Sheila had ready. I'm unprepared. It feels right and wrong.

Their short story is written here: there had been '*misconduct, intimacy*', an offer of marriage, later withdrawn. Billy had asked the navy to pressure him but he disappeared. Until now. Is it finally him, the man who made me, or is he legend for Barnardo's to make my adoption more agreeable? Have I found the one person I wasn't looking for? Is the gap too real to feel? I leave with my notes neat in an elasticated file.

Next stop a London address around the corner where the records say my mother had once stayed. I never knew she'd been in London. Her side of Valetta Grove, a stunted Plaistow street, is now a park. Her plot, number 3, is a rubbish tip, chained up and high-fenced off. It feels like an omen. By the time I get off the tube in town my legs are weak. A fuse lit long ago has finally blown.

MARCH 20. Spring equinox, the day I may have read my father's death certificate. There is a Francis O'Toole, killed at 26 when I was three, run over by a car in Kirkdale, Liverpool. He died of shock and cerebral laceration, a fractured skull. A labourer's short life snuffed out. Misadventure, the coroner says. This Francis O'Toole has the same name, the same age but it is too early to say if he's mine. I need more time for more research. All I know is the pain it must have brought his family. For now, I want to get lost, feel soil under my nails.

Branch Hill is bathed in sun, warm enough for sowing. It is a leaf day. I put out jute string, green today. I cut short sticks. I weed, I hoe, I rake. I mark out eight short rows, divide seed into groups. Howard arrives. I stop for a while. A kestrel flashes by, very low at head height. It feels like benediction. It flies into the border trees above us, sits framed by the blue sky. Its feet readjust their grip on a skinny white branch. Its head bobs, turns and watches, scans the site. Its feathers puff in the afternoon sun. Its markings are clear, its wild profile perfect. It sits still, silent, as do we. Suddenly it swoops, fast, flies to us, banks steeply and turns less than six feet away, like a fighter aircraft flypast, a sort of salute. We watch as it flits from trees, sectioning the site, eyes alert. It knows this place. Finally, we gather seed, drop packets by the rows. A coloured chard here, a coloured lettuce there, companion planting with my good companion. For a long moment I feel lucky. We water in, we sow. We shift chervil. The sun drops. The air cools. There is time for two last rows across the middle. Fast-growing rocket to dissect the space, a signal of intent. It is spring, the sun is on our side. I hold to the healing.

MARCH 21, SATURDAY. I am sitting in an intensive therapy workshop. Twelve other 'adopted adults', a 'trainer' and me. The session is about finding your birth parent and what happens then. I normally wouldn't have come, not my thing, but the invite landed in my inbox two days after my sisters' stories. I didn't know what to do with the information, lovingly given, of how my mother gifted her children to men. My fellow therapees are mostly veterans of the workshop circuit. Their sad stories come easily, though there is real hurt and rage. Voices choke,

there are many tears but not mine. I don't feel the connection. Maybe because I am the only man or maybe because
I wasn't part of an adopted family, I can't feel part of
theirs. It is a long day. I am exhausted. Most of the group
want to go for a drink and carry on while they can, share
their stories with people who understand. They want to
meet up again soon. I want to go home.

MARCH 22, SUNDAY. It's the allotment spring-clean
working party, time to tackle and finish the pond. I have
brought sharp knives and pair off with Bill, my
early-morning friend. We trim the excess plastic and dig
a ditch around the perimeter to bury the edges in. We
stop to watch frogs watching us, heads alert and eyes
intrigued. The 'old' pond is alive with excited movement,
oblivious to anything but spring and spawn. They are
overcrowded and need more space. We move in the
marsh marigolds and uprooted iris. As summer comes,
the edges will blur and blend. People come to admire our
work, ferry buckets of muddy water. Ian goes home to
get the key that turns on the mains supply. The pond fills.
The frogs might just forgive us. Two barbecues are
topped up. There is soup burbling on the stove. Someone
is grilling chorizo. We sit in the early-year sun and bask
in joining in for the joy of it, communal jobs well done.
Mary is here and other faces unseen since the last growing season. David has brought pink prosecco. He is
pleased with the revival of his plot. I steal away to sow
calendula. It is early but I have hope. I have been here
four or five hours, getting muddy and happy. I haven't
thought about anything else.

MARCH 25, WEDNESDAY. At work. An email has come through with another copy of another death certificate for another Francis O'Toole. I'd first ordered in copies of marriage certificates for the five I could find in the UK who'd married in the 10 years following my birth. Better to gatecrash a wedding than intrude into grief. None, though, were the right fit. I am now, hesitantly, looking into the dead. One had been a baby, another the young man knocked down by a car; now it is the turn of Francis Anthony O'Toole, who died at the Royal Liverpool Hospital in November 1984. His death is registered by his brother Christopher, who had been with him at the time. I like to think they were holding hands, that perhaps there was peace. There is a birth registered for Christopher in 1936 and his marriage to Margaret in 1961. They are on the electoral roll at the same address given when he registered Francis's death. I feel a bit faint for the office as I write to him. I don't say why I am looking, just that I am. A first-class stamp and it is done. I have a sneaking feeling for this Francis I am trying to suppress. It might be because he had a brother called Christopher. It might be because he had lung cancer, but I feel disturbed (welling up, close to incontinent crying) as I return to reading proofs.

MARCH 26. It's our wedding anniversary. I am cooking. Plans to eat out are put on hold as Henri is working late. Christy O'Toole calls from Liverpool. His brother Frank was in the navy for nine years, he says. He was a cook based out of Plymouth. He was the right height. His name and age and size, his place and occupation all match. I think I may have found and lost my father. I only had him for a day. I couldn't help but be excited at the thought of seeing him. We would meet and eat if he'd wanted. Drink beer and talk late into the night. He would share stories about ships and family. He would tell me about meeting my mother. He would talk to me of how it was. I would hold on to him for dear life if he wanted, my dear old dad.

I couldn't help wanting my father. Christy is warm and welcoming. I tell him why I've written. He says a woman came to his parents' house once searching for Frank. She stayed a few days. The brothers showed her Liverpool. She left a photo when she went away, but Frank tore it up when he returned.

Frank was one of 13 kids, he says, an Irish Catholic potato-famine family, though only four are alive. I say I am sorry to disturb him. I am trying to put together pieces. His mother had never said anything about a baby, he says, but he would talk to his older brother and see what they could find. Frank's wife had died recently, 30 years after him. He had been a heavy smoker: navy cigarettes. He liked a drink. His children loved him very much. It is good to hear.

He will ask if they have their father's discharge papers. See if it says anything about serving on HMS *Decoy*. He will find a photo, have a copy made. There's one of Frank in the navy. He will call me when he sends it. I like this man. After we talk, I finish preparing the food. I wish Henri was here. I'd like to mull it through with someone who may understand. I need to lie down while I wait. In minutes I am fast asleep. It's not yet 8pm. When Henri comes, we go to bed. We will talk it through in the morning. Our anniversary is on hold.

MARCH 28, SATURDAY 8AM. The allotment. The boards arrive for Mary's walkway. Howard and I carry them to the plot. It's too early to fit them now and the weather forecast isn't good. The allotment is covered in sycamore seedlings, which seem to have sprung the same day. There are too many to pull. Howard takes the long-handled hoe, while I use a hand tool to cut in close. Order is restored and the wild repelled. I return to beautify the pond, which still looks a little industrial. I wander the site perimeter gathering logs and bits of bark. I wrap them around like building a wooden bridge. I am looking to soften the hard edges and naturalise the space. I top up the level with water. A stubborn frog sits on a lily leaf as it rocks up and down. I have brought calendula to sow: pure orange only, English old-school. I sow nasturtiums in the gaps beneath the boardwalk. I have been thinking a lot about my brother Christopher lately. I am looking for a riot of colour, something exuberant in gypsy tones. Common, like foster kids.

MARCH 29, PALM SUNDAY AFTERNOON. I have promised Mary I will attack her pumpkin pit. I lug grubby sacks of horse muck, spacing them apart. It is raining. The border trees shake in dramatic gusts of sudden wind. I wish I was wearing waterproofs, not corduroy. It is muddy gardening but there is comfort in the discomfort and I can't stop now. There is a job Mary needs doing. It is why I am here. Soon enough I am soaked, but the pit is ready. I am satisfied. It's too wet to sow, so I weave in more wood around the pond and watch more frogs. I stop in the Catholic priory across the road from home.

The statues are shrouded for Holy Week. It's the Desolate Church when God is dead. I pick up a few strands of palm and light a candle, I'm not sure why.

Celts and cooks and my mother: what was it with her? Christopher's father appears in my Barnardo's notes. His name is redacted – so she didn't say Ray – but he was, it says, a navy cook, same as Frank and Ray. The first three fathers of her first three kids. There is a rule in journalism: three is a 'thing'. One of the reasons Frank seems real is that he was connected with food. It's the area I have built my later life around and a safe place when talking to my mother. But how did she meet them? How did she know? Did they have badges, like in the scouts? Was there a chefs' corner in Union Street: a bar only cooks could drink in? I wonder what was the quality that attracted her. Was it nurture, was it appetite, were they good with their hands? I wonder if they knew each other.

1967. I discover French butter when I discover French kissing, in Isigny Sainte-Mère. It's twinned with Kingsbridge. I am on a school exchange. It is the summer of love. Normandy butter is pale and sweet, not the New Zealand salty yellow brick we have at home. French cheese is ripe and runny. It smells of life and farms and shit. The kissing starts in the cinema. I am sat at the back. She lets me slip my hand in her shirt, clumsily stroking cupped lace, kneading her breasts like bread. She doesn't slap it away as it runs up her thigh. This is a first for me. I don't recall her name now but I remember tufts of hair, blue Gauloises and yellow Gitanes, Johnny Hallyday crooning Hendrix. I ache to be experienced. She is

patient. She wears a girdle. There is no way in. She laughs
and puts her urgent tongue in my mouth, my first taste
of an unpasteurised life.

April is the cruellest month, breeding
Lilacs out of the dead land, mixing
Memory and desire, stirring
Dull roots with spring rain.

T S Eliot, *The Waste Land*

APRIL

APRIL 2. There are photos on the kitchen table. Three of Frank. The first as a young man in a group of grinning sailors. He is bossing the centre, his arms the only ones crossed. The other photos are much later. The confidence has faded. An older woman has her arm on his shoulder. She must be his mum. I like the look of him. I want him to look like me, like my dad, but he doesn't. My hopes had been building. The useless need to belong. I am unsure what to do. The simple answer is DNA but I don't know if it is what I want. After a lifetime of uncertainty I am comfortable with it now. DNA seems final. I am used to feeling my way. Christy O'Toole calls late in the evening. I tell him I can't see Frank's face in mine. He says his daughter has Googled me and I look like his father. I cling to that. He hasn't told the rest of his family, he says. We are both taking small steps, edging towards something.

I think I want to visit Frank's grave, talk more to this Christopher. There are tombs for unknown warriors, for those who lost their husbands, fathers, lovers, brothers, sons. Maybe Frank can be that for me: my unknown sailor father figure.

APRIL 5. Denmark. An Easter of sun and sea and spotted woodpeckers. We arrive at the summerhouse to see a pair of sparrows moving into the nesting box. Their beaks meet as though kissing through a window. We wait to get out of the car. We walk the long way round the house. They have arrived at the same time as us and are bound to be disturbed. We spend the next days going in and out by the back door.

A flock of chaffinches is combing the grass for seed. The primroses have spread through the border and clustered around the trees. Wood anemones are scattered at the back and south of the plot. The cowslips are coming. The hepatica are in full flower through three borders, migrating more than ever before. I lie a long time in the leaves to admire them. Spring is almost here. Hedge birds chorus from before 4am. I could watch them all day. A pair of spotted woodpeckers follow each other up trunk after trunk, hopping in search of hollow. The male stops and drums out a Morse signal. Four full days of sun, of walking the beach, of eating outside: smoked mackerel on rye, horseradished herrings, fish soup from the northern seas. The blackbird alerts me to leaves in the guttering. I add them to the compost pile. It is happy work. Perhaps because of Christopher, I've decided to add a bed of calendula, more domesticated than our usual wildflower planting: sentiment in sowing. The grass is growing again, dotted with daisies and yellow celandines. I spot pockets of white and blue violets. The place is perfect. I wake. I light a fire. I make tea. I stay away from the phone. We are outside all day after breakfast until the cool evening breeze drives us in. We wrap warm to watch the sunset: slow-moving cloud, magenta sea and sky.

April

APRIL 7. Allan O'Toole to add to my portfolio of personalities, other kids who were nearly me. Can't help wondering who he'd be. Would he have been happy? Would my young mum and dad? Would Frank have felt trapped by a momentary mistake or would he have made the best of it? More importantly, would she? When and where did it go wrong for my mother? Was it the lure of men, a sort of revenge? Was it the miscarriage at 17, being spurned by Frank and Christopher's father? After her third failure in three years, marriage to Ray would have to work. Perhaps it was chemistry, perhaps a Christian thing. Only Ray knows now and he's my Howard Hughes. The answers he is looking for are eternal, he tells himself. Mine are more immediate. For now I will quietly try on Allan O'Toole like shiny new shoes and wonder what his life would have been. If he'd still be like me. Allan Beale, Alan Jenkins, Peter Drabble, Peter Jenkins all still swim in my memories. I get out Peter to talk to Lesley. He is a comfort to her and to me. Allan O'Toole feels like dressing up. I'll wrap him in tissue paper and place him in the drawer with the others.

Barnardo's notes

7.4.54. re Allan Peter Beale. The above mentioned little child has been accepted for admission for adoption and I have allocated him to come to your branch. I have asked that you are advised direct as to the date on which you may expect the infant to arrive and have mentioned to the applicant that if the journey is made via Oxford, you would be willing to send someone to meet the escort at Oxford Station if notified of the time of arrival there. As Allan is coming to us for adoption, he should in addition to the usual ration documents have with him a full copy of his birth certificate.

7.4.54. re Allan Peter Beale. With reference to my letter to you of the 18th February last, I am now pleased to tell you we have an immediate vacancy for this little child at our branch known as Oakley House … I cannot find that you have yet informed us of the type of food to which Allan has been weaned and I shall be glad if you will kindly ensure that a diet sheet accompanies him to our branch …

City of Plymouth
Maternity and Child Welfare

8th April 1954

Dear Mr Webber

re: Allan Beale

Thank you for your letter of 7th April and your kind promise to take this child into your Abingdon Home. I am arranging for the child to be sent on Tuesday next, 13th April and have notified Miss Talbot Rice accordingly.

Dr Barnardo's Homes. Branch: Oakley House. Beale, Allan Peter, was admitted to this branch April 13th 1954. A cross should be placed under the name of any article missing and the form returned to Stepney immediately. Please examine ration documents and repost any defects and see whether the name on the identity card is the same as the one sent from HQ.

Name: Beale, Allan Peter. Age 15.1.54.
Admitted 13.4.54
Height 23 inches. Weight 13lbs 10oz
Appearance and demeanour: contented.
Cleanliness and general care: fair
Marks of violence and injury: no
General condition: good
Muscle tone: good
Skin and hair: skin rough, thin, scurvy
Genitals: N
Nervous system: apparently N
Skeletal system: N

Three months old in an orphanage. Newly separated from my young mum.

Appearance: contented. Even this early, my saving grace.

Skin and hair: rough, thin, scurvy. A shame in one so young.

Skeletal system and genitals: N. Normal then and now, I am glad of that.

Nervous system: apparently N. Almost a title for a journal. Appears normal and still is. Apparently.

APRIL 9. Last visit to the plot before a two-week trip, the guilt kicks in. I tell myself I am going to sow a quick row of salad seed but really it is to ask permission, like from wife or priest or parent. Let's call it absolution. The pond has failed. Holes have appeared in the lining. We will have to drain and start again but we try first to patch it like a bicycle tyre. Frogs are sitting in the thickening water. Ruth is muttering about sabotage. For the past two weeks I have been weeding sycamore seed, the terminator germinator. The rocket is up, most of the 'leaf' rows are showing too, the first calendula is in a clump, and at last the broad beans, hopeful leaves like rabbits' ears thrusting from the ground. Spring is fast turning into early summer. A last furtive look over my shoulder and I sneak away.

The first time I really cried after my mother's death was in India. A couple of months late. I was travelling through the north in search of temples and tigers, staying in a lodge inside a reserve. I couldn't sleep so I sat by the Ram Ganga river. The moonlight was sharp, a deer was standing chest high in the running water and I found myself crying; for my mother's loss, not mine. I wondered how the young wife in her wedding photo had morphed into the woman I met. I didn't yet know the depth and darkness but I could see something essential had been lost. I sat on a stone on the edge of an Indian river and I cried, for the hopes she had, the life she might have lived and for the damage she had done. Now I am back in India, with my brother on my mind.

April

I hire a rickshaw to the city to buy jasmine for Henri and marigolds for Christopher. It is Vishu, the first day of the Keralan calendar, a good time to say goodbye and scatter flowers like ashes into the sea, the ceremony I missed. I stand on a large rock at sunset as waves suck the sand around me. I try not to slip. I throw handfuls of marigolds into the water. I tell him I love him and think of him often, that if the Indians are right and he has another chance of life I hope he has a mother who will never let him go, a father who is supportive and proud, and a brother who won't turn his back. I watch the flowers swirl. Marigolds wash up on the sand, most are carried out. A message in a bottle: Christopher David Jenkins, born Beale, RIP.

13.4.54. Appearance and demeanour: contented.

From the baby days in Barnardo's, so it appears, I was content. Blindly trusting, like a near-newborn kitten, I would be OK. Take me from my mother, my brother, I will make the best of it. Hold me occasionally. Feed me. I won't cause a fuss. I will be quiet and loyal. Be yours.

14.4.59. Plymouth case conference. Boys to be divided to find foster homes.

24.4.59. Both are delightful little boys and have lovely little sayings and ways of expressing their pleasure. Both children are also well mannered and very fond of each other.

The decision is taken to divide us. To split us in two, though the notes talk of how we both cling to the brother we barely knew. It is one of the things I despise about Barnardo's: how siblings were separated. It wasn't enough they had 'lost' (as though mislaid) their parents and identity. The last link to their family was also snatched in the glory days of philanthropic gratitude. Christopher and I were too much of a handful for one family, the anonymous voice writes, two troubled small boys. I wonder now if Christopher would have been happier if I wasn't there? Would he have been doted on or would he have been left alone in the children's home? I think I leached his love, appropriated his lovability as though there wasn't enough to go round – and in truth it was in short supply. I wonder what would have happened to me without having him. We were each other's broken teddy bear. Would we have found each other later, would we have wanted to? Would I have looked and longed for my mother, found Lesley, Ray, my other sisters and brothers? Later Lilian and Dudley were to try to split the litter. No more room for the runt.

> 30.4.59. Replied to Mr Drabble's letter, no definite assurances could be given regarding the children remaining in care but it would appear they were not wanted.

'Not wanted'. Days after the dividing decision, Lilian and Dudley Drabble had a look at us, bought us on approval like I used to with stamps. Take us home and try us out, try your luck. Fairy-tale old folk in their fairy-tale thatched house who gave me back my brother.

April

Two weeks of sunsets over the Arabian Sea. Sleeping to the sound of crashing waves. Watching fishermen sing as they pull in nets. Walking holding hands with my wife. A fortnight mostly free from Christopher and Sheila and writing. My past parked in long-stay, while we get on with our lives. Old memories have been mostly happy: of walking beaches and rivers with Tessa, swimming in the sea. Chris, skinny-legged in shorts, with his big ginger grin, trying to avoid sunburn, being calamine lotioned, painted chalky pink. Perhaps there was an ice-cream wafer or a sandy sandwich with Sandwich Spread, maybe Dairylea. I've been reliving early days with the Drabbles: shooting with bows and arrows, trying on a happy family. I think I am letting Christopher go a little now. He's mostly only been here when I have invited him in. I buy more temple marigolds for our last sunset, say a soft goodbye and watch them wash away.

APRIL 27, 7PM. It has been warm while I have been away and the plot feels impatient. There is a run of broad beans on the south side, green, with multiple leaves. The potatoes too have spread. The red mustard has spiked a foot in a fortnight and is flecked with yellow flowers. The chicories have doubled in size: full, fat, lush and ready to eat. The baby salad rows are prey to pigeon. Early summer is being born, though the forecast warns of frost. I soak it in like the sun to someone with SAD. I pull more sycamore seed. The site is closing in now with lime-green leaf on the border trees, shivering with life like newborn lambs. It is dotted with sweet-scented apple blossom, cloudy carpets of forget-me-not. I feel more like a boy here than anywhere. I sow a mixed row of peas, one for shoots, one for pods. It is good to get my hands grubby. A son of the soil. I leave with fennel fronds in my pocket. A kestrel shrieks goodbye at the gate.

APRIL 28. I have booked train tickets and a hotel in Liverpool. My heart in my mouth. I cannot admit even to myself how much I want Frank as my father and his grave as a resting place. It is tough to believe it might be true. Sheila couldn't be trusted. I fear it's another blind alley. There is no place left after this.

I am resolved to DNA. It feels unreasonable to appear without proofs. It is not that I need it. I don't, I think. I would take it slowly. There is another responsibility, though: to them. For now, I'll spend the day with Christy O'Toole, see if he recognises something in me and I see something in him. I will accept his hospitality. I will visit Frank's grave but I will ask Christy if it is OK that we don't rely on my mother. It's not that I am looking for closure, I don't think it exists. Some wounds scab over, then weep without warning. I am an Iceland of magma. I occasionally erupt.

In the difficult nights as a child I lulled myself to sleep by listening to my breathing. Christopher rocked back and forth, determined if slightly demented. Now I hold to Henriette. Even her hand seems to work.

1967. We practise kissing in circles, four on four, moving clockwise every two minutes. I am 13, learning secrets from a sexual world where people exchange spit. The first step is to learn how to breathe, no drowning, gurgling noises. We have five minutes with each to get a feel for each other and a taste of technique with tongues. Each subtly different, subdued, eager, impatient. I am besotted with S. She is adopted. Has already had sex. I obsess about her black underwear under her white school shirt. She has swagger. Her boyfriends have scooters or cars. They know how to unleash a bra. No way I can compete. She can't be seen with me. I am sometimes allowed private lessons at her home while listening to the Monkees. We might be lying down. There might be wiry, sticky touch. She is an indulgent teacher. But I'm not old or dangerous enough. Our first sex is on someone's kitchen floor next to the cat food. We'd met again at a rock concert. We'd smoked a couple of joints. She is wearing a maxi skirt, a floppy hat. She smiles as she opens her legs. I won't see her again for 20 years. She is the only bright light in a class reunion. The early promise hasn't worked out for most. There has been divorce and disappointment. Faces are stained with bitterness. S. is sporting silver hair. How are you, I ask. 'I've got a Porsche,' she smiles.

APRIL 30. The last day of April, the first morning of sowing before work. I am excited, up early after India. It is still a little cold. The hill is covered in bluebells, blazered children are being ferried to expensive schools. The shallot shoots have spread like green fingers; happy onions and garlic are lit by the morning sun. I am dressed for work so I take off my jacket. I spot a baby radish the size of a fingernail, a perfect gardening perk. There are a couple of clumps of autumn-sown chard, their scarlet stems showing well. I join them with a short row of candy-coloured beet. Flower, leaf, fruit and now root: the first spring sowing's done. I pick mustard leaves and chive flowers, bronze fennel bushy like a foxtail.

MAY

MAY 2. Return to the Danish plot. We've caught the tulips at their best, rare at this time of year. There are runs of reds standing straight like soldiers. A naturalising yellow like a large buttercup is almost over. The wild cherry trees are in full blossom with delicate, fragrant flowers. Translucent leaf screens the site like a watercolour, softly blurring the boundaries. We wander round in wonder. The house can wait. Cowslips stand tall in the meadow; I cut them before Henri mows. We mix them with cherry blossom, like dressing a church for a spring wedding. I rub my face along the larch, the new needles soft as a kitten. We sit on the terrace, silver birch stark against the sky. This is the slowest burn of my growing places. It is mostly about trees and bushes, creating space for wild flowers to make a home. Here is land we subtly shift to bring in light, build painterly corners. The espalier pears are all in bloom, waiting for the bees. The apple trees too are covered in bud. For two long Scandinavian days the sun shines, we eat breakfast outside, barbecue sea trout from the bay, walk along the empty beach. There is still a threat of frost in the night. I light morning fires. There are no passing cars or sirens, just a background hum of birds and waves. The supermarket is selling half-price seed like a pusher outside a school. I buy too many packets. We are planting bulbs from the lily of the valley bought for Henri's birthday bunch. My days are peaceful but my dreams disturbed, I am again surrounded by dangerous men. In my bag there is a DNA kit and train tickets for Liverpool. It is uncertain what they'll bring. Until then I have poppies to sow and grass to lie in, beautiful escape.

Our days in Denmark start with a pyjama walkabout, sometimes with a coat, fleece, hat and scarf, thick woollen socks. I wander down the lane like this in hope of seeing neighbours' anemones, stalking feeding deer. Mostly though we patrol the plot's borders, looking for new life and new blooms, new bud in spring. We watch it fade in winter. It is here we will see the small changes, spot the spread of wild lupin, see how the blackbirds have a nest in the hollowed birch. It is on these walks that we get a feel for the life outside our interventions. I spend hours *watching*. Time drifts like smoke from the stove.

MAY 5, 7PM. Allotment. Large, lazy wings, a prehistoric profile: I arrive at the allotment to see a grey heron being chased by a crow. It had been in the pond, hunting small frogs. There are hundreds now. The crow harries it off site. The heron doesn't want the hassle. It is another evening visit after work, soundtracked by birdsong. I have been carrying seed all day in among papers and printouts I need to read. I have made up a mix of American amaranth and an unusual sorrel. I have added

Danish lettuce. I'll mostly crop as cut-and-come-again leaf. A fox appears a few feet away, looks at me unconcerned, a little curious. It's young, its coat almost fluffy. It trots slowly past and suddenly jumps with puppy surprise as though it's seen prey. It roots out a pair of leather gardening gloves. Another time a fox stole one of my shoes when I had changed in the rain into wellingtons. I found it later, chewed and abandoned, unsuitable for work. The fox rolls around on the ground. I should perhaps interfere, save the gloves. I move towards it but it grabs one and runs. It is darker now. The woodpecker calls. I leave content, the antidote to office life, old anxieties, even anger – infallible as always.

MAY 8, FRIDAY 5.40PM. Halfway to Liverpool. Trees flash past, toy-town houses, fields, roads, rivers, horses, hopes. I feel uncertain. This trip has been looming for a few weeks now. The accused waiting for trial. The condemned. The upsides are obvious: perhaps a father, a family, though 50 years late. Anxiety has burrowed under my skin like scabies, whispering fear in my ear. I feel like a kid with Christopher. I wish they were all still here: Frank, even Sheila, my brother. I have the DNA kit in the bag beside me, mocking me with my hopeless hopes, for what, for fuck's sake? It is all long lifetimes away. I am not the editor facing north but almost the same boy as on the train to Paddington meeting another father in another time; or the 33-year-old going to meet his mother. You'd think I'd have a handle on it now.

I change at Crewe. The rain is insistent. I am passed by a carriage load of close-cropped men in too-tight suits;

big-hatted, clingy women in clinging dresses, returning from the racetrack. Not long now till kindly Christy O'Toole – this my first and likely last journey unless the kit proves me wrong. I can't help but hear Sheila's witching cackle, her last revenge on foolish men.

They are still a mystery to me, her and Ray, relics from another time, belonging in a gothic novel: a raddled Johnny Depp could play me, a busty Joan Collins my mother. I am close now. An emptiness like hunger. Runcorn, Acton Bridge, the fields are waterlogged. My fellow passengers are working on their laptops, reading phones and magazines. Their weekend starts here. This time tomorrow I will be heading south with my swabs in a bag. It is hyper real, a parallel universe, now moments away. Liverpool South for John Lennon airport, Lime Street: he will be waiting at the station, my name on a card like at an airport. Except there is no sign saying Allan Jenkins; no answer on his mobile. He isn't home. I need to pee but daren't leave the platform. I wait 20 minutes. I try the taxi rank and the other exits. It is a sprawling Friday evening. People with places to go. There is a neat, elderly man also waiting. I catch his eye, look questioningly. He looks away. How long to wait is long enough? I try his mobile phone another time. I re-call his house. Has something happened? Has he changed his mind? I have to leave. The old man carefully unfolds a piece of paper – Allan Jenkins. He has been waiting on another platform. His timing was confused. I shake his hand. Rain is hammering down. We go to the hotel. We eat in the restaurant. He insists on paying. We drink spirits and talk till late: my story, his story, his brother Frank's. I want it to be him but DNA hangs over my hopes. The next day we visit Frank's grave, except Christy doesn't know where it is. It has been 30 years since he was here: he goes to funerals, not graves. There are thousands of headstones, many with fresh flowers. I call the cemetery helpline: it is Liverpool City Council out-of-hours, the Saturday service. The tape plays looped music, all their operators are busy but my call's important, it says. No chance they'll know where Francis O'Toole is buried. We leave.

Sitting in his son Paul's conservatory, I show them the Barnardo's records with Frank's name, occupation, his navy barracks and ship. He reads them quietly. Paul looks me over and says I have the O'Toole eyes. The same pale blue, agrees his wife. I have been scanning for noses, mouths, chins, facial features. I may have missed the eyes. It is always the eyes with everyone. I suspect there are maybe millions of us. There is only one way to be sure. Christy and I swab the inside of our cheeks anti-clockwise for a minute. We label the DNA envelopes carefully.

Paul reads out the Barnardo's notes: his Uncle Frank's character is 'indifferent'. Sheila's, he reads, is weak. Our pale blue eyes well up. I try hard to hold it in. I had somehow forgotten how poisonous the papers are. Later we meet Christy's eldest son. He had worked with Frank, he says. Being his nephew and Christy's son had meant he was accepted easily. They are gentle with me, the Liverpool O'Tooles. I am fragile like cracked china.

Christy and I take a ferry across the Mersey and look at the liver birds; we visit The Beatles' Cavern and take in the city sights. Too soon I am back on the train heading south. I wonder if I will see him again. He says we will stay in touch whatever the test says. But it's not possible, I think. Back home, we examine photos of his father and grandfather. It is there in the eyes, says Henri. I blow them big and compare with photos of me. It might be possible. I walk to the post office and place our DNA in the box. It will be a long five to 12 days. The murderous nightmare returns that night, the door in the dream fast shrinking in the frame as I struggle to keep attackers out.

MAY 10, SUNDAY. I am unsettled. My internal world is shifting like disturbed stones in a pharaoh's tomb. As ever, I head to the garden centre. We are there a long time. I am indecisive like Alzheimer's. We gather trays of geraniums, poppies; too many for the car. I follow in a taxi. It takes a lot of flowers to quiet my anxious inner voice. While Henri fixes pots and window boxes, I go to Plot 29. Mary is there. She is looking stronger. Her broad beans are tall and in flower, her wigwams already up. I weed carefully in the sun for a few hours to give the small salad leaves a chance. It is good work: husbanding and nurturing, encouraging baby plants to grow free of being smothered by choking weed. The plot looks full of promise for summer, pea shoots and beans are shyly poking through. I am grateful for this place, for my patient wife who has planted the pots and swept the roof ready for me to cart the rubbish out.

This much I learned about Frank in Liverpool: he passed his exams for grammar school but, with 13 kids, the family couldn't afford the uniform and books. His eldest daughter was a day off 21 when he died. He never married their mum. He was respected in his telecoms job. He was never late, always early for work. He was to be found at 7.30am, sitting doing the crossword. He liked to drink. His chosen pub was a Yates Lodge, his drink of choice white wine. His brother Christy went to his funeral 31 years ago but has never been back to his grave.

MAY 13, 6.30PM. It has been hot, I have been hopeless, torn between two worlds, neither fully formed. My identity feels fluid, memories bubbling up. They were kind to me in Liverpool, the old man and his sons, but it's been sucking my breath away. I have spent my life building in love. I believe in sticking and staying. I won't repeat my mother (or father), I tell myself. Now I am demolishing my security brick by brick, searching for the shaky foundations and sand on which I am built. It is relentless now. I am in the shadowy basement of my life, throwing light into hidden corners and tearing out rotting wood. I turn to the plot for relief. Late sun casts church-window light through the greening trees. I pick about, thin the too-tight rows, potter in peace. There is no one here, just a robin following where I'm watering. Heavy rain is forecast so I figure it is me that needs the life-giving can after can, row after row. We eat my salad with supper. I feel happier for the first time in days.

MAY 14. A note in from the DNA lab. All arrived and all in order. The results may take another two weeks. My heart flips when I see the message in my inbox but I have to wait.

MAY 17, SUNDAY. A sunny afternoon back at the allotment for my repeat prescription. I arrive to a flurry of noise. A duck is being chased by the fox and barely makes it over the gate. A few minutes later it returns, loudly indignant. I am worried for it. It scours the trees and makes a lot of fuss. It flies in repeated circles over the site. The fox may have stolen its eggs or attacked its young. I wish for its sake it would quiet. I dig up the remaining chicory, leaving three tall plants, leaves fanned out like a flamenco dress. The soil is the colour of coffee grounds against the fresh green growth. I rake and even the slope a bit, admire the iris breaking through the grass. It is our only perennial flower, nestled in the bank next to the fast-spiking sorrel. It is delicate, quietly coloured, found at a rare plant sale. Mary is here when Howard arrives. Our three gardeners reunited. We have decided to replace the path and planks on Mary's end of the plot but leave the shallower end uncovered. I have been liking the way the buttercup has been colonising the bank. We will let it run free, not a time to tame it. There is another explosion of squawking. The fox misses the crazy duck by a couple of feet. Again the bird barely escapes, while the predator hangs by its front legs on the fence.

MAY 19, TUESDAY. My extra month of therapy is over so we decide to continue week by week. I started coming here in the anxious aftermath of reading my Plymouth records and now it seems my search is shuddering to an end. I have no more avenues to explore and no more appetite for pain. Christopher's grip on me is loosening, or so I tell myself and her. I am still unsure whether he's hanging on to me or it's me holding on to him. He is dead. It is finished. No more to be done, just a few more questions to be asked. Maybe I will never be totally free or want to be. Will he always be aged six for me, broken by my mother? Will he always be a kid with his lopsided smile? Will I always be sorry? Now it's just me and his memory. I want to hold on to his fading. I want always to give him wild flowers and tend his marigolds.

MAY 20, 5.30PM. I am on the bus with Howard on the way to build a bean wigwam. A pregnant woman gets on. I give up my seat. Sitting at the back, I open my phone. There is an email from the DNA lab. My results are ready. For a few moments I imagine waiting. I should prepare, I half-tell myself, and open it at home. I had thought I was free from hope for a father. I've been proud to stand alone. But I have broken through to emptiness like an undiscovered cave, with giant ferns and rivers, herds of animals, a million bats. How to miss something you never had – who knew it was possible? Normality is a powerful tug, my desire to pass on simple goodness, not my mother's toxic blood.

Client Ref: Jenkins
Test Results – Peace of Mind

Dear Allan Jenkins
Enclosed with this letter you will find a copy of your test results. We understand this can be a nervous time and it's important to take a few moments and breathe gently.

Whether the results are what you had hoped for or not, please take the time to consider how you will move forward rather than reacting to the news which may cause you to say or act in a way that is not your true feeling.

If after receiving the results and considering your options you would still like to talk to someone, then the organisations below may be able to assist – we are also on hand to answer any questions you have.

I open the attachment. There are two pages of matching mathematical equations, solving a theorem: the mystery of me. I skip to the end, the answer.

Relationship Test Certificate Case Reference Number: P024167

Sample No: HID150513_014 Alleged Uncle: Christopher O'Toole

born 06/09/1936

Sample No: HID150513_016 Child: Allan Peter Jenkins

born 15/01/1954

DNA isolation was carried out separately for all samples. Genetic characteristics were determined by PowerPlex 21 PCR Kit (Promega), Investigator HDPlex PCR Kit (Qiagen) and PowerPlex Y23 PCR Kit (Promega). In parallel, positive and negative controls were performed which gave the expected and correct results.

We were requested to find out if Christopher O'Toole is the paternal uncle of Allan Peter Jenkins or not.

Based on the genotyping results, we compared the following two hypotheses.

A: Christopher O'Toole is the paternal uncle of Allan Peter Jenkins. The father of Allan Peter Jenkins is a full sibling of Christopher O'Toole.

B: Christopher O'Toole and Allan Peter Jenkins are unrelated.

Due to multiple exclusions on Y-chromosomal markers, hypothesis A is genetically impossible.

The bus climbs the hill. My stop next. But my legs are cut from under me. Will they wobble? Will I fall? Teasingly close, now snatched away. Fuck. Fuck. Fuck! Sheila slithers in her undead grave, smiles, satisfied. Howard looks to me questioningly. My chatter's choked. My smile sickly. There is a sister of a friend come to stay at the house. No way to be alone. I need a cat to cuddle, a duvet to hide in, but next best is building a garden structure with hazel poles. The plot feels friendly. We sharpen the ends of Jane Scotter's sturdier sticks and hang on to push them in. It is near impossible not to grin. We will transplant the beans later but the wigwam is soon up and tied with twine. Howard picks salad. My appetite is shot. My mother. Christopher barely three months old, her third pregnancy, still living at home with her mum and dad and brothers. Breastfeeding and sleeping with Frank, and at least AN Other. My father. I feel confused and conned. I can't bear to call Christy O'Toole. I need a rest from the rollercoaster.

It has been sitting there for 60 years. In a file on a shelf in Stepney. I should have worn protective armour. The same with the Plymouth records, information gathered like the Stasi, secrets collated. Information so explosive it must be handled with care. I have been working on this bombsite for more than a year now, trying to make it safe. It was always likely go off at any minute, whether from Dudley's dangerous thoughts, his bitter whispers or demands for more money. The fiction about Francis O'Toole though was a sophisticated device waiting patiently for me to pass by. Sooner or later luck runs out. I cannot even pretend this was for Christopher, no shelter behind my brother. This was simply me and my missing. A child's need drowning out any other adult voice. I am back now where I started, square one, minus a fresh injury. I heal quickly like a jump jockey, bones, heart sometimes broken but spirit mostly intact. I am happy with my life, my beautiful wife, the people who love and need me, the work that makes me happy that others seem to appreciate. It is mid to late May in my year of gardening and childhood, my communion with Christopher. The right prayers have been said, the priests have left, now it is just him and me saying goodbye. Like the last time I saw him and told him I loved him. I was his brother. It has always been enough for me, mothers and fathers were for others. I had him, he needed me and so did his memory. I have stood on the precipice and recited his name.

MAY 22. I call Christy O'Toole. I have been sitting on the DNA results for two days now and it has to be done. It's probably the last time and the thought makes me melancholic. He can't quite take in the news at first and gets it the wrong way round. I think we were seduced by the romance – him for his long-dead brother, me for a father I'll never know. He tells me they've been planning my next trip. I tell him I'm grateful for his kindness but here it ends. I wish him and his wife and family well. I wish it were different. I wish it were true. It would have been good to have loving in my line. But it's the Samuel Beckett oblivion ending. We will keep in touch, we say. I will send him a Christmas card.

MAY 25. Denmark. The swans have gone, the swallows have arrived, lining the electrified wire to the Icelandic horses' fields. The young males are impatient as the females call. Like a boy band, their long hair hangs over their eyes. The first foal stands unsteady on skinny legs, its knees too big, its coat curly like astrakhan. There are marsh orchids in the field. I climb over the wire and admire the marking. Skylarks flutter impossibly high. Their call echoes inside me. Wild lilac in every shade lines the hedgerows. We ride through its fragrance on our bikes and pick an armful for the house. The larches seem to have grown half a metre in a month. The wild carrot and campion sway in the slight sea breeze. The birch stands spectral in the evening light. The bird cherries are forming, food soon for migrating flocks. The blackbirds call from their nest in the hollowing stump. The hare, huge now, runs through, up on his strong back legs, a flash of orange back. I thought he was a fox at first but nothing else moves likes that.

We have walked by the waves at sunset, wrapped against the northwest wind. The sea turns tarnished silver as the light drops. Here I am inoculated against my missing father. Blossom covers our apple trees. The three pear trees all cross-pollinated. We sow tulip seed because we can afford to wait three years. It is a place for families. We mow the grass. We watch the wild things. We trim the beech, weave branches back. My back and shoulders are moaning, I have been stabbed in the eye by a stick but the firs are standing free. We sow foxglove seed in the cleared space. They will take two years. The last tulip petals hang off their stems like flags at a bedraggled bandstand.

MAY 25, 7PM. London. Time for a quick cup of tea after the flight, but the homeless beans are calling. I lift the nursery row, plug beans around the base of the hazel poles and push in an occasional seed as backup in case of marauding slugs. The broad beans are flowering crimson, black and white. I snack on a few top leaves as a treat. Howard's away so I sneak in a few sunflowers in the corner. The plot seems to like the attention. The salad rows are bright green and red in the gloom. There are a couple of us working quietly in the late-light summer evening, only looking up to nod or say hello. My mourning is over (at least for now). I am looking forward to the longer days.

At home I find notes I'd made after talking to Colin in Melbourne. There's another song he thought I should hear. This was for the Sheila he knew. It sums her up, he says. It is a disco song from the Eighties, featured in *The Adventures of Priscilla, Queen of the Desert*.

> Please don't talk about love tonight
> Please don't talk about sweet love
> Please don't talk about being true
> And all the trouble we've been through
> Please don't talk about all the plans
> We had for fixing this broken romance
> I wanna go where the people dance
> I want some action, I wanna live
> Action, I got so much to give
> I want to give it, I want to get some too …
> Alicia Bridges, 'I Love the Nightlife'

It was through music I first learned there were more like me, just not in Aveton Gifford. The shaggy-haired boys on *Top of the Pops* (I identified more with the Rolling Stones than The Beatles; I yearned for a Marianne Faithfull). Later, when I moved around, music was a shorthand to my tribe. The introspection of Leonard Cohen coloured my studies at Battisborough School. The death of Jimi and Janis added doom to Basildon days. Magazines, too, played a part. *Oz* and *International Times* exposed a world of sex and drugs. The Isle of Wight Festival in 1970 (Hendrix, The Doors, Sly and the Family Stone) ended my childhood. I slept on the beach outside Ryde for three weeks, only going back to Basildon to say goodbye. I didn't yet know where I belonged but I knew it wasn't among skinheads or to be found in Ray's preaching. For a year or few, I drifted through empty buildings and ley lines, swooning to Van Morrison with floaty girls in green silk. By the time I was 18 I was squatting in London, running an occasional hippie cafe offering two courses and tea for 10 pence. I was happy guerrilla gardening around Notting Hill Gate.

MAY 31. John is fixing the new super-strimmer. He strips and reassembles it from scratch. I cart Mary's sacks to the compost. She is here a lot now. I empty bags of manure into her pumpkin pit and rake it around. The muck is almost liquid. We are at the time when the plot seems to shrink, and I don't yet have enough of anything except for rocket. I borrow the strimmer to clear the connecting walkway and break it almost immediately. I have never quite mastered the mechanical thing. It is approaching 8pm when I leave. I have been here the whole weekend. The path and plot are cleared and so is my head. I am grateful for the chance of finding my father and family but I have been good (or good enough) without it all my life. Recovery comes quick, I tell myself.

JUNE

JUNE 1. There is a text from Tony O'Toole. He writes that he is Frank's eldest son and 'received information today that there was a possibility we both had the same father'. He hopes I don't mind him contacting me.

I wish it were true, I reply, though the DNA says no. I call him later. We speak for an hour. He was around 17 when his dad died. I can hear the loss in his voice. He talks lovingly of Frank. Towards the end, his kids wheeled him to the pub in the evening and picked him up at closing time. Frank never knew he had cancer, Tony says. His mother wouldn't tell him.

Tony has re-read my Barnardo's notes five times. He can't stop going over them. He has Googled me. I have the O'Toole eyes. He thinks Christy's leukaemia treatment could have affected the result. It might have been the blood transfusions. He has always thought he had a big brother out there, he says. Family legend has it that Frank carried a photo of a boy in his wallet and that Tony's mother had found it. His dad was a cook and I write about food, he says. He wants it to be true. I feel helpless. I might hang on to shredded hope but DNA doesn't lie. But it is in the eyes, he says. His wife agrees. I can feel his need overriding mine.

JUNE 7. Howard is here for the working party. He is back from a week in Wales. He is with Nancy and Otto, their new puppy. We move the last comfrey barrel and measure the support struts for Mary's boards. We take over the barbecue. John sings Irish songs under the apple tree. His sweet tenor calls The County Down. Mary looks content and caught in conversation. Most everyone joins in.

Later that day, I phone Christy. I am concerned about Tony. I am messing with his memories and am unsure what to do. Christy has heard the story about Frank and the photo. It couldn't be you, the boy was blond, he says. We resolve I'll do a test with Tony to put his mind at rest. We will use a kit Christy had bought. He will send me one of the swabs. I text Tony to tell him of the plan. I don't want the uncertainty but it seems the thing to do. Then this is the end.

JUNE 12. There is an allotment letter from David's wife. She says his dementia has advanced from early stage. He keeps wandering off to the plot and leaving the tap running. She has told him it's time to give it up and has handed in his key. She asks us not to let him in, as locking him out is the only way. The good news, she says, is he forgets quickly and comes home jolly. It is not in his nature to be angry. I will miss him and his old stories of Africa. I am not sure I will lock him out. His plot already returns to weed. Someone new will make it grow. I hope they keep his asparagus bed.

JUNE 13. I can't stop thinking of Frank and the photo of the blond-haired boy he carried around. Before the days of DNA, he would have thought Sheila's child was his. It is a tradition for soldiers and sailors to run away but he could have kept in contact, at least at first. Sheila may have sent him a photo of his son. He may have kept it. There is a curious comfort in the thought he would take it out to look at it in Yates Wine Lodge or as he travelled. The memory of his unknown child somewhere, a moment held half alive.

JUNE 14. There is a new bench on the roof terrace; a new rose and tomatoes too. Here I walk around in bare feet, dead-heading and tidying. There is often a baby robin at the feeder now. I try not to disturb it as I move. There are heavy-headed poppies, scarlet as a soldier's uniform. The Alexandra rose we bought when Lesley's son Justin died is pale pink like wild. For the third year there are tomatoes. From Jane Scotter seedlings. She has stopped her stall in London. I miss her inspiration but she has been unwell. The tomatoes have been staked and the leaves picked out. I am obsessed with their smell when I brush against them: ripe with memories. That is all they are now: Lilian, Dudley, dear Christopher. I tend their remembrance still. Mostly, though, I drink in this space like spring water. Something alive without legs to look after. A quiet place above a London street, with the power to lull me to sleep.

JUNE 19. Another envelope with my DNA in the post. Another man with a hole where his father was. I hope he'll be OK, Tony O'Toole, when science shuts down his dream. Thirty years after his death, Frank and family can't escape. Sheila's rage echoes through decades. Her hand snakes out to trip us up. We fall like dominoes.

Last on the list is Ray, sheltering in Basildon, incanting denial. He believes he is protected by Jesus, forgiven, safe, that he somehow escaped. For a year now I have thought I would have to confront him about Christopher. But I don't believe in avenging angels. He is no Eichmann, after all. It would have been good to know. It would be still. But will I go and ask him, turn up at his door? I am less sure.

It has been a year since I started this journal, my journey through my life and the life of the plot, my past unfurling like leaves. It was to be different: a story of a small boy and the man he became, wrapped in flowers and food. Other voices have drowned it out: the call of an insistent brother; sisters still scarred from abuse; the voodoo cackle of my mother. Characters have changed, like wrongly labelled seed producing unexpected fruit. A kindly father figure reveals a crueller side. An ill-suited foster mother becomes gentler with the patina of time.

When the journal started I was recovering from an absence from the garden. The plot felt abandoned (of course), sullen and needing coaxing before it opened up again. Boxes of documents almost blew the writing off course. Meticulous records from a life in care: my bloodline pored over by committee. The Barnardo's notes were still loaded with secrets, armed with my mother's childlike signature. Still unsettling after 60 years, latent like anthrax spores.

Over the year the plot has given up broad beans, yellow beans, blue beans, green beans, purple-podded black beans; pink and white waxy potatoes, peas, radishes, endless salad combinations, beetroots in many shapes and colours; corn, kale, chard, herbs and flowers. Nasturtiums still give succour, coloured saffron like Indian robes. The flow of food like memories sometimes threatens to overwhelm, though easier to conquer than clotted fear. There are woodpeckers, blackbirds, robins, wrens, the kestrel calling, hovering a few feet overhead. There are hordes of frogs and magical newts. There are John Teevan, Annie, Bill and Ruth. There is American Jeffrey, with his English garden. Closest, of course, dear Mary and Howard. There is a plot of land the size of a living room where I have found companionship on my own.

I am happy surrounded by the trees I have planted by the sea in Denmark; with my tomatoes, rooftop roses and other flowers. But there is an older welcome on Plot 29, like a feral cat I come to feed. Bring me your fears, your anger, your endless packets of seeds and I will give you food and flowers and peace. My dull lead shines golden. Simply put, there is a home in homegrown.

JUNE 20. It is midsummer now, time again for bright, early-morning visits to the plot. We have blackfly on the broad beans and I haven't the heart to spray the organic exterminator sold in the garden centre. It's not that I have qualms about killing blackfly. I hate the way they suck the life out of the plants they infest. But if soap was enough for Lilian, it may still work for me.

I raid the kitchen for eco-friendly washing-up liquid and catch the first bus. The flowers and baby pods are crawling black. I spray soft, soapy death down on them. It is the aphids or the beans. I pick a pod for encouragement. I add more soap to the spray. It's someone's time to die.

After I finish, I water. The hose ban is still in place but husbanding crops sits well with me. I return later to gather onions and shallots. It is time for chard to settle in before the sun starts to dip. I sow four short rows of different colours: white-stemmed, rainbow Bright Lights, pink and gold. I finish with dill, coriander and parsley running the length of the path. I have been here for four hours. I thought it was two. One last trip on solstice Sunday, up with the sun. I'd spotted a few tagetes that I thought had failed and it's an auspicious time to sow more. I add a row beside them, and another at the end. They should be good with autumn beans, courgettes and corn.

I want to reclaim my childhood from the records. I want to override facts. I want Dudley to be the kindly dad I constructed, not the mean-spirited man I unearthed. I want it to be summer in the early Sixties. I want to be coming in from playing on the river for buttered new potatoes and runner beans. I want Lilian to be smiling. I want there to be Angel Delight. I want Christopher to be excited about a new calf being born. I want him to score a six. We weren't the pristine girls Lilian had wanted, the pure-born sons Dudley craved. They weren't the hugging parents we'd hoped but it wasn't in the job description, this twenty-first-century stuff about love. We were happy before Mum and Dad's disappointments set. I want to remember the bright nights in bed in the crowded caravan that summer when the sun always shone. I want to erase Dudley's begging letters to Plymouth, his anger and honesty. I want to rediscover the joy of the flower seed he gave me. I want to see nasturtium grow. I wish I didn't know what he felt in bitter detail. I want my happier memories to block out the wretched whispering. I want my mum and dad back. I want them to want me.

JUNE 27, SATURDAY AFTERNOON. Back from a few days away. The blackfly are being herded by ants like the Masai moving cattle. Where are the ladybirds when I need them? Their numbers are down.

I am here to stir biodynamic cow manure, the building block of our soil. I sit on the steps by the tool shed, roll up my sleeves and swish mucky water to and fro. The sun drops and the energy shifts. Someone has borrowed the brush I spray with, so I cut a swathe of sage.

I am back in the early morning, meaning to sow late flowers, but I have left my seed bag in the rush for the first bus. I move sunflower seedlings, feeling for their spot. The dill is a still-shy, hazy run of green. The chard, too: scarlet-tinted, tiny. I weed. I water. I gather an armful of white-stemmed Fordhook Giant chard, its savoyed leaf a deep-forest green. I have brought three kinds of red tagetes seed from Sweden. Howard takes photos. The French beans look happier, holding on tighter to the poles to pull themselves up, whether revived by cow muck or the morning rain.

There is an anxious note from Tony Walker. It's about my DNA. It takes me a moment to realise who he is. Tony O'Toole, my just-possible brother and new Facebook friend, also uses his mother's name. Another man with another alias. I wonder which one he feels like. Anthony Walker on his birth certificate, Tony O'Toole to his friends. I wonder if it is confusing sometimes, as it occasionally is for me. His mail says the DNA lab needs my signature before they can test whether we share the same dad. I sign the authorisation and email it. I will know the answer in a couple of days, though it will more likely tell me who I am not than who I am.

JUNE 30. 'I didn't marry your mother, I married Christopher.' I am in a room with Ray. I have been putting off going but I am drawn like a moth. I need more understanding of what occurred in the dark ages between birth and Dudley Drabble.

Ray is the keeper of the secrets: my life from Barnardo's baby to a four-year-old sheathed in sores. He is the mother lode, the father who knows though has never said.

I am back in Basildon. Kids are streaming out of Woodlands, my skinhead school. It is 32°C. Too hot. I grab a cab. I ring the bell of the bungalow. The little house is wrapped in roses. I wait. I ring again. I knock.

A thin voice calls from inside. I am coming, it pleads. A slow shadow moves, then there he is. The man who married my mum. I don't recognise him. He is heavier, older, with long, sickly, sticky hair, a ragged Don Quixote beard. He looks questioningly at me. He doesn't know me either. It's Peter, Ray, I say. I hold out almond tarts from Patisserie Valerie. Peter, I repeat – my name as a teenage boy who'd lived with him for a year. He looks bewildered. It's been a long time.

Peter? Peter? Allan! He finally says. A thin smile. I follow him in.

We sit. He eyes me warily. The room smells of age and illness. I start by thanking him for sheltering me as a baby and a wild boy with nowhere to go. I make reassuring sounds. I mustn't spook him. Like stalking a wild animal. There is much to ask. How long had he known my mother when he married her? Why did he do it? What was she like? When and why did she leave? Is he Christopher's father?

The stories come slowly at first. He gets confused, he says, he can't remember. Most of what he says doesn't add up. The years are wrong and the timing out, we weren't where he says we were. This is the first time he has talked, but he is 87 now, maybe his memory has gone. Maybe it's hoarded and buried.

He starts to talk about Sheila. He knew her brother Terry, he says. He'd go round to the house.

I wasn't interested in sex, he says, I was interested in Christopher.

I felt sorry for him, he says, he needed someone to care for him. He used to come up to me as I was coming up the path. Half the time Sheila was never there. She was out down to Union Street.

While he heats his homemade dinner I ask were they ever happy. Not what you call happiness, he says. It was convenience for Christopher. I don't know that it ever did come to anything.

I ask if there was anything nice about her? She was very friendly with everybody else, he says. I caught her with a bloke under a couple of trees. You get down home, Sheila, I told her. And you clear off, I said to him. They both stood there. She said, you clear off, I am not taking your orders. They didn't move. I had to get back ... Half an hour later, she turned up.

Apparently sometimes she didn't even know the bloke. Sheila was something I shouldn't have done. It happened and that's the way it goes. I am still here.

His friends had tried to talk him out of it: I had a good mate, he says, joined up the same time, tried his damnedest, said you are being very silly, I don't think you ought to marry her. Give it a bit longer. But who is to say what could have happened worse if I hadn't married her?

He starts talking about the '[Jimmy] Savile business and Rolphy [Harris]'. Half the time, he says, the women and judges are just as bad.

I have some experience, he says. I couldn't have been more than seven. There was a young lady, I know she was 13, she used to take me to a field and get me to play with her. Later, she went up to work at a gentleman's house as a maid and got pregnant.

He tells me about a girlfriend. She was oversexed, he says, though they 'were never together like man and wife'. They always had separate rooms when they went away.

A couple of years ago he got the greatest shock of his life: I had an older sister lived with my grandmother. I always wondered why they called her Betty Jones, he says. When I was 82, my brother told me she was born before mother married.

He tells me that when he was in Plymouth a neighbour asked to adopt me 'and she meant it. You were a bonny baby'. He is tiring now. I won't get any more about my mother: why he let her take Christopher away or why she brought him back. I have drawn a blank on my brother, on cruelty and sickness, the crucial stuff. He has locked it away and I don't have a key. I thank him and call a cab. I mustn't punish my brain any more, he says, it's getting near my bedtime.

The taxi pulls out, the summer evening falls. It is all too late, too long ago. So I leave him to his bungalow and his loving daughter who looks after him. Leslie Ray and Lesley. I think I wish him well. It is only when I am close to home I feel I may have been played.

JULY

JULY 1. The day after Ray. The new DNA result is in. It's 98.7 per cent sure Tony and I share the same father. I don't understand it. I don't know how I feel. The last test said it was impossible, and I am (almost) reconciled to Frank not being my father. I didn't dare hope, did I? Tony texts to ask if I am OK. I don't know. It must be a mistake. How can it be? Is this really it? What are the percentage chances that these results are wrong?

I can't talk to Christy O'Toole. I can't talk to Tony. I have to check. People's happiness depends on this. Mine among them. Do I send another sample? See if it matches the one they have? My feelings are suspended. Did Tony somehow mess up the swabs? I would almost rather lose my sense of family than the old man lose his. If Frank is my father, how can I be unrelated to Christy? Their mother is a Mother Teresa, the sacred rock on which the O'Tooles are built. I don't want to be her undoing. A late, kindly act for a stranger over a letter and Christy's world could fall apart. He is nearly 80. He has leukaemia. His wife's had a stroke.

I take a day, head and heart slowly spinning, then I call Kate at the DNA company I used with Christy. I read her the results, ask if they make sense. Is there another way to interpret it? Could they have been corrupted or even engineered? I hate the suspicion. It is as though my happiness has been stolen or at least misplaced. There is no joy in Frank, in finding my father.

Kate says from what I say the test sounds good. She would trust it and she's an expert. It would take a sophisticated operation to fix it. And why would anyone want to? It is just two men testing where they belonged as boys.

JULY 3. I write to the second lab with questions. Did they test for full sibling or for half? Could one person's sample have been tested twice, might they have made a mistake? Should I send another? I haven't spoken to Tony. I don't know what to say. Texts are too inadequate for something this size.

JULY 6. Three days late, I call him. I apologise for my silence. I tell him I have been too confused. I can't stop thinking about what it may mean. He says he has felt the same. We talk about Christy and Frank. I say I have written to the lab. I need to know more before I know how to respond. He says he sent three samples, two of his with the one of mine. My hopes softly sink into Devon sand. I ask, why would he do that? He says someone told him to send more. I ask him to call the lab on Monday morning, tell them to recheck he is not 98.7 per cent certain to be related to himself.

JULY 7. The allotment. I need to think. I need peace, blackbird song and soil. I take a spray for blackfly that we keep for flowers on the roof. I can't stand the life-sucking any more. Now the pole beans are infested and the nasturtiums too. Their tendrils and leaves hang limp. There are large patches of parasites. I spray. I repeat. I spray again. It is not biodynamic.

When I finish, I feel sick from the killing frenzy but the eco liquid wasn't working. I don't stay. I don't sow seed. I feel corrupt. I wish I could rewind but how far back would be enough?

Maybe it's over, this year of deep digging. For what? Was it for Christopher? Was it for me? What did I learn? I feel infested with life-sucking fear. Anxieties are flooding back. The capped well is leaking, the stink has returned, therapy like eco-liquid too weak to clean it away. Maybe it needs an Agent Orange. Darwinist Dudley Drabble, Pentecostal minister Ray, my mother Sheila, Doctor Barnardo's, Plymouth 'care' workers: a plague on all their houses. It is time to stand on my own again. Fuck 'em. They were unfit for purpose. Sometimes I think Christopher and I would have been better off if left in a box.

Christopher! My deepest regret, my darling, nightmare, beloved brother. I have stood inside this furnace for a year pleading for forgiveness. Now I am granting myself parole.

JULY 15. Wednesday morning, allotment, early. A leaf day. The weekend's summer storm has washed away my pre-solstice seedlings. The sun rises a degree or two closer towards its wintry shelter now. The blackberries are firming. The dahlias are coming. I carry a change of clothes. I step out of my office shoes and wander round the plot filling in gaps. I sow red and green salad. The French beans are leaping up, released from parasite prison. I sow nasturtiums in the bank and add a few tagetes. My life is nearly back to where it was. A blood-ied soldier coming home. There are fresh wounds. I am carrying shrapnel. I have been struck by shade. Whatever it was, it was worth fighting for but I am retiring. Just me and the seed and soil from now. I hope here's where I'll stay.

JULY 17. The Liverpool lab says it's satisfied with the results. I still feel withdrawn. I am confused why I can't celebrate. What is holding me back? A month ago I wasn't aware of doubts. I wanted Christy as a father figure. I wanted a connection with blood. Now I am on the threshold, I am unsure I want to go through. Will my new fractured family's needs leave room for mine? I am daunted by the idea of new brothers and sisters. I will have twelve siblings. It is impossible.

There is a fear, small but stirring, that behind the door lies something secret that hurt me when I was young. In the other areas of my life I have built in safety. I keep my back to the wall. I watch the doors, keep an eye on the windows, see who comes and goes and when. Here, though, I stand naked as a newborn.

I fear a connection to chaos, a loss of control. A runaway car I can't drive. A hill, no brakes, a wall, a cliff, a thousand-yard drop to rocks. An oblivion I once would have welcomed. A loss of self built from scrap. Tony wants a big brother. I have been that boy before for Christopher and for Lesley. That man for Caron, Susan, Michael and Mandy, my mother's brood. We will do another test. I am almost ready to turn the key.

JULY 18. The tomatoes are doubling in size every week and showing yellow. The roof terrace is turning too. The roses are taking a rest before a last late-summer show. The lobelia's almost over. The days are drawing in. It has been quite a year for the flowers and for me. Occasionally we look a little tired.

Dudley is the only dad I will ever have, though Frank may be my father. Dudley protected me, moulded me, helped shape me to the man I am. I am deeply aware of the debt.

I love him dearly and miss him often; I am looking at nasturtiums in a jar. But, oh, what was he thinking? How could he plot to split up Christopher and I? Was it like a gardener thing? Weeds and the weak to the compost. Stronger plants to shelter and sun. We had been a family. Christopher and I had cleaved together at the children's home. We'd been conjoined, almost twins.

We came as a pair, like pots. Love doesn't tear you apart. Doesn't hack off limbs. I won't always be angry about it. I wish I wasn't now. The Plymouth box will be put away. It has been tough to digest the decade of Dudley's thoughts. I want only to remember Christopher contented on his lap. I wish my dad had hung in longer. We had a contract. I had taken his names. He had made his mark. We would be his sons. He should have picked me up from Battisborough School. It was his job, not a social worker's.

I get that it was hard to stick with. But he had taken me in, he should have taken me back. He could have seen Christopher thrive, loved his kids. He could have been a granddad. He would have been good at that.

In the end we shouldn't have grown older. We shouldn't have grown up. But real life's not really like that. There is no Never Never Land. No lost boys, no Hook, no Wendy. I was Peter Drabble not Peter Pan.

JULY 19. Driving back from the country, I can't wait to see the plot. The weather has been hot. It will need me. It is getting overgrown. Howard is not here to crop and pick, and I can't wait for him any more. I lift potatoes – Pink Fir and Ratte. I cut lettuce and three types of chard. I will carry the onions home. All the high-summer garden crops: potatoes, peas, leaves, with beans coming soon. The squash at the back are starting to spill down the bank with the nasturtiums. I will move corn and sunflowers into empty space. Time to cull calendula, sow chicory, kale, late-summer salad. I need to clear for autumn. The black cat watches as I water. The light drops more obviously early now.

I pan for more memories of Christopher but the seam is mined out. Everyone's moved on. It's a ghost town now. I never got drunk with my brother. He never spent the night. I never made him breakfast. We never ate together in restaurants. Never had fish and chips. I will never walk with him again by a river. We will never look out over the sea.

JULY 20. I almost can't believe I am doing it but I have asked Tony to take another test. He will post his swabs from Liverpool and I'll send mine from home. They will be put together and tested at the lab. A last spin of the family wheel. Is Frank the father I wasn't looking for, found when I lost the one I had? Pandora's box isn't empty. Hope hasn't flown, though Nietzsche says: 'Hope is the worst of evils for it prolongs the torments.'

JULY 21. Up at the allotment at 6am. Wednesday. A work day. It is cool. It is crisp. The light is lower. I am being bitten. I fork up new potatoes, dusted with earth as though by a stylist for my magazine. I clear the peas. I strip the pods. I place food in a bag and hang it in the shed for Howard. The pigeons call of the country. I clear beds for seed. I hoe. I rake. I compost. I sow chicories and chioggia. I collect horseradish leaf for a Ukrainian friend. I water. I wish I could be here all day. It is urgent but it will have to wait. I need to be in the office, I need breakfast, a bath, to wear a suit. There is a posh lunch later. It won't taste better than picked peas. Later, a call to Plymouth to one of my mother's brothers, my Uncle Tony. I am wondering whether Terry really was Ray's gateway to Mum. He would have been 16. Tony tells me he and Terry didn't know any sailors at the time. He says he can't remember when Ray appeared. Tony lived with Sheila while Ray was away at sea. She used to cook his lunch to take to work. He tells me about Sheila coming home from hospital the day Caron was born. She went straight out, he says, to Union Street. Not one for rest or maternal instincts. She was a one, my mum.

JULY 22. Time to call my Uncle Terry to talk about Ray. Whether they were friends before he met my mother. It is not how he remembers it, he says. He thought Ray met Sheila in a dancehall next to the navy barracks, just before rock 'n' roll. Terry was courting Barbara. I can hear her quietly correcting his memories. In those days, they say, there was the Embassy Hall, the Labour Club and St Johnston Social by Devonport dockyard, where sailors met with local girls. They saw Ray there a couple of times and on the docks. Terry says he and Barbara visited me at Queen's Gate, a residential children's home. I was maybe three. Sheila had left by then. I was there on my own, he says. He doesn't remember where Ray or the other kids were. They took me out for a drive. He had a Ford Eight at the time. We had tea at his mother-in-law's. I was very blond. They have a photo of me from about that time, he says, they will find it and send me a copy. They have never heard of Francis O'Toole. Sheila had a lot of secrets, kept them to herself, they say. I thank them for their kindness. I would have been glad of the day out, I think.

JULY 24, FRIDAY AFTERNOON. There is an email in my inbox. The DNA results are in but I can't make the password work. I panic. Do I really remember it? Is it a sign? I call the lab. The word is confirmed in lower case. I open it. I want it or at least I think I do.

There it is. Confirmed. I have found my father. The hypothesis that Tony O'Toole is my half sibling: 98.72 per cent probable. There is quiet release. Relief. Understanding will be slow but the secret is exposed to sunlight. There is an ending. I think it is happy. A new seedling to protect. Tony took my hand while I stood blinking. His faith strong, mine myopic. Nearly Allan O'Toole, father Francis. The birth certificate is no longer blank. I don't know what it will mean to have eight sisters, four brothers. Too much to take in but there is time. First will be photos, names, more information. Tony says he will send them in the post.

I go home, then to the allotment. It is bucketing torrential rain. I clear overgrown summer leaves. I want to be ready for winter. I return twice over the weekend. I empty Mary's sacks of weeds. I watch the pigeons feast. I prepare new beds. I move plants around. I spray stinking comfrey tea. The replanted corn will need it, the summer squash, too. I cut courgettes, and flowers for the table. The green woodpecker calls. There is just the plot, my plants, my memories. I will nurture them.

JULY 29, EVENING. Christy calls. Tony's youngest sister Bernadette had asked to come round. She wouldn't tell him what was up on the phone so 'a bang had gone off in his head'. He knew it was about me. He knew it was the test. He didn't understand how the new result could be. I tell him I hadn't called because I wasn't sure what to say. I tell him I'd had the test double-checked, then we'd done another with my swab sent direct from London. There was due diligence. It seemed it was sure Frank was my father, or at least 98.72 per cent. He says he wished he was my uncle. I say I wanted it too. He's now going to do another test, he says. He wants to know if Frank is his brother. I tell him I am sorry to be the cause of this mess. DNA was supposed to bring certainty, answer questions, not ask more. I can't celebrate finding my father yet. Somewhere I am still unsure.

AUGUST

AUGUST 16. I take a call from Tony: the family has a theory involving an unmarried aunt. Perhaps she had a child, maybe Christy or Frank, who had been taken in by their mum. Their mother's reputation stays intact, maybe more saintly than before.

AUGUST 18. My sister Susan posts a picture on Facebook: my brothers Christopher and Allan, it says. It is from the day we met our mother. I am skinny in my early thirties and corduroy but it is Christopher I can't stop looking at. He looks happy, standing tall. There is a big grin on his ginger-bearded face (I didn't remember the beard, how it suits him, only later with his military moustache). Dog tags hang around his neck. This is the brother I have forgotten, the one obliterated by the boy and the dying man. Here he is reunited with his mother at last. He belongs in a way I never will.

My smile is my photograph face, my slightly nervous mask. His is wide open and trusting. This is what he has waited for. He had been with Sheila until he was six. I didn't have the same history. We had been interrupted.

August

This is a good time for him. It is the only photo from the middle years. He had finally found his family, ready to be wrapped again in her bosom. The warm milk of belonging, her mothering love. I will add it to my memories. The moment when his future shone.

SEPTEMBER

SEPTEMBER 5. The allotment salad is seeding, beautiful, semi wild. I am overwhelmed with beans now Howard is away. The Swiss chard and chicory are set for late autumn. I weed around to give them air. I pull beetroot as big as a baby's head. The sunflowers will bloom soon. I will leave them for birds to feed.

The pigeons have decimated the Tuscan kale. Mary's tomatoes are blighted. I carry their corpses to the wheelie bin. Summer is nearly over. The plot colours are cooling. The red salads are rusted like old tractors. I pull the tallest and strongest, and lay them in the cold frame for seed for summer. It has been quite a year.

SEPTEMBER 6. I walk on the outside on pavements. Old-school good manners, I told myself before I wondered where it came from. I sit on the left side of buses. I cannot sit with my back to the front of a train. I walk the same route around Hampstead Heath. Sometimes I reverse it. I am a creature of habit. I need to know what the day has in store. I don't think anyone taught me to be on the outside when walking. There is a scant memory from a children's home of walking in twos, I don't know where or when.

It is a mantra of repetition – the same walk on the same side, the same seat. I think I maybe built my neural pathways from early on. I constructed my own memories. In the absence of family, I crafted the familiar from the unfamiliar, found comfort in the cold. It could be that it is like OCD, repetition in a quest for safety. Perhaps I feel more vulnerable than I like to admit but I will go with politeness for now.

SEPTEMBER 7. A call from Tony: the new DNA confirms Christy as his uncle: 99.8%. He and Christy are happy, he says. I am content for them too. I don't want to carry my mother's contagion, her family-eating plague, but I can't see how it computes. If Christy is Tony's uncle, can Frank still be my dad? A couple of days later I call Christy to congratulate him. I had thought to ask whether we should retake our test. But I hear the blessed relief in his voice and I haven't the heart.

I know my mother, he tells me, the woman she was. The uncertainty had plagued him, I think. For him and Tony the search is over. Right's returned to the O'Toole world. We talk about the importance of family. Of its measure of a man. You are both my nephews, he says. We'll have a meal when you come up.

I guess that is the next step, to meet Tony, my other Michael, my four O'Toole sisters. I tell myself I wasn't seeking certainty. I think with goodwill we can paper the cracks. Maybe I can be their elder brother. Maybe Frank can be my dad. We will tread carefully. It looks like it isn't over yet. The fat lady hasn't laughed.

I can't find my humour in my writing. It's not how I'd tell my story if we had wine. Laughter is how I neutralise hurt. I turn it into a tale, make it funny, make it mine. Here, somehow it is still solemn; my wife's a little worried it's not like me. Melancholy has settled like river mist. I tell myself it is temporary, it will be burnt back by the sun, I am still tunnelling, making my escape. I should be free of it soon.

Fathers and brothers. Men and boys. I had pined for the company of women and girls, for my mother, for much of my life. Men were tougher to get close to. I'd thought my longing for a mother was because Mum felt less loving than Dad, but history shows it isn't so. It was easier to love Lilian when she was out from under Dudley. She was gentler company, light to Sheila's shade.

I had a brother, a father, a few close male friends. I was comfortable with making myths. I must be nature, not nurture – my 'real' dad the reason I differ from my siblings. Where did the greed and ambition, the words, come from if not from him? I wasn't looking for specifics. I had thought to trace my tribe.

He'd been a fantasy figure, my father. For a brother I had Christopher: my conflicted relationship with boys and men in one. Pull, push, pull, push. Push. Now I have four new sisters and two brothers, five of them friends on Facebook. Perhaps they will bring me closer to my father in a way I couldn't be with my mother. For my O'Toole clan, I am a link to their dad, reliving his life before they were born, his love before he was lost. Maybe it's not my place to be a child finding his mother and father but to be a big brother to them all. It is what I do, what I have always done.

Mothers and daughters. Women and girls. Lilian pined for an adopted daughter but Dudley insisted on sons. Too late for their own, he picked up a pair second-hand, slightly damaged with wear and tear. Lilian fed us, read us stories, walked with us to school. We were sent to church. She purged us of Sheila's sin, nervously scrubbed at the stain. Puberty, of course, was impossible. We were past our sell-by date. No one buys pubescent boys except maybe my other mother. Sheila had cornered another market where everything had a price. You could buy on approval, lease if you liked. Satisfaction or money back.

I haven't had the hunting dream for a few months, though I still sometimes wake, heart thumping, adrenalin pumping, as though I have escaped. For now at least, knives are sheathed, sitting somewhere maybe, waiting in a bar, behind a blind corner – who knows? I'd like to think it is over. Decades of being prey is long enough. I wonder if it was processing terror, doomed to repetition, reliving a moment over and over until it fades. But there was no diminishing of the dream. One day it was there and now it is gone. I don't know what it means, my silent night. Have my hunters moved on or are they still lurking in my shadows? Night time will tell.

A year in the garden. From summer to summer. From green growth through dead winter, back to life. Leaf, flower and fruit, lush moments before the fall. We have had rain and sun and snow. There have been towering sunflowers, bean structures, amaranth swaying in the wind. Wigwams have gone up and fallen. Poles have been put up, taken down and packed away. There have been many kinds and colours of lettuces, beets and radish, other roots. Fragrance has flavoured the food we have made, rosemary, fennel and thyme. We have roasted homegrown corn on site, cooked Mediterranean soup. Winter-sown onions, shallots and garlic are sitting in my kitchen waiting to be fashioned into autumn meals. There have been many successes and a few failures (the fragile-plant stockade, raining death down on parasites). Whatever the weather, I have been there. I have been too cold, too wet and too hot. I have hoed. I have been bitten. I have weeded and watered. I have nurtured and nourished small plants through their short life. I have been constant. I have shared food and flowers and saved seed for another year.

I don't know what I would have done without it. The healing would have been slow. When I have been troubled, when I need to be alone, it has been there for me. I care for it, I coax it. It has forgiven me for abandoning it when I had a broken leg.

A year in the life. Summer to summer, one father to another. Through gloom and despair and back. Digging land and memories. Throwing away rose-tinted thinking. Shining light in forgotten corners. Starting with an homage to an old man, then seeing him in high definition, the full 360 degrees. From loving him, losing him, to loving him less, though this is likely temporary. Reading and writing about the two boys. Trying to deal with the facts. My mothers: one scary and skinny, the other monstrously fat. Both falling short. Hearing stories from my sisters I will never be able to share. Dudley and Christopher, the two towering men in my life. Both absent for long years. Now both dead. Trying to please

Dudley, taking his name. Trying to please Christopher and taking his too.

A year of putting them both to rest. A time of trying to find peace through the truth. A return to therapy when I was done with it. A time of toxic boxes about a life in care that wasn't. I am ready to put them away.

Finally talking to Ray. An invisible, unreachable nearly-dad whose name I will always bear. Discovering more about Allan Beale, his baby months in an orphanage. About Alan Jenkins's sicknesses – his stigmata signs of neglect. A year spent calming a scared little boy. The one to wear my too-many names. Time spent with Peter Drabble, forgiving his treatment of Chris. Feeling relief I am not him any more, though I have grown to like the kid and his confidence, like a fast-built Chinese city towering over the swamp he once was.

It has been time to let Christopher rest. I have found a place where we can grow marigolds and nasturtiums year after year.

I will take a breath before exploring Allan O'Toole. Meet his brothers and sisters, dig for their memories of another dead and distant man. Open my dusty closets. See what fits and what's to go to the charity shop.

A year of gathering thoughts, strength and information. Peeling layer after layer. Holding back tears, trenching for laughter. Hunting for happiness on a riverbank. Putting everything back in its place, cleaned and dusted. Grime, grease and cobwebs gone. For now there is a contentment, hard fought for, perhaps, but won.

A year older. It couldn't wait any longer. They are dying around me. I limp. Reclaiming who I am. Who my brother was.

This year has been my ghost train, a fairground trip on a slow boat without oars. Ghoulish figures, luminescent with menace. People from my shadows, archetypes of fear: the sexually voracious, monstrous mother; the absent stepfather; the cupboard under the stairs; the hell-fire preacher. Predatory men flashing blades and cocks. Through the shade, a Peter Pan boy on a mission, to escape, to save himself, his broken brother and sisters. There is light now in the tunnel, the ghosts are exposed as painted ply. The cobwebs cling, but they are fake. The fears and memories shrink as they recede. The sticky hands are less insistent.

DECEMBER

In Loving Memory
Our dear dad and granddad
Francis Anthony O'Toole
Born 13th June 1931
Died 28th November 1984
Aged 53

DECEMBER 4. Thirty-one years late. He is long gone. The flowers I have brought from London lie under the new headstone he shares with Irene, mother to his other children, who died last year, November 29, the day after him. Tony has left me alone for a few minutes to make sense of it, to try to feel something.

Here he is at last, Frank my father, the dad the baby craved. This the man whose genes I share, lying in a box under Irene in the Liverpool earth. Memories now for others, a skeleton figure I am here to flesh out. The wind rips at my coat. I changed three times before I left home. What to wear to meet your dead dad and your new brothers and sisters?

Trees shake, flowers lie blown in the grass. The gusts pull at me. I am cold. I try to conjure knowledge from the stone, from the chrysanthemum and carnations, from the green glass pebbles that cover him. I try to feel him, let him feel me. Would he have been happy I am here? The Barnardo's baby would have wanted to stand at his father's grave. I get into the car with my brother. It is time to meet his wife.

The Blob, in Liverpool, once Yates Wine Lodge, a sprawling room with rows of tables for four. Old men drinking Guinness and lager with the same friends in the same chairs for, say, 31 years. Only the name over the door has changed. Frank drank Scouse 'Aussie white', not Chardonnay. Brown like sherry, 17 per cent proof, it's sweet and flat like yesterday's Tizer, served with ice and topped with lemonade. It is powerful booze for working-class men and women and people who drink on a bench. I can almost see him here at the table with Tony, Mick and Bernadette.

Micky 10 Tops, his kids call my kid brother. He is always cold, his hand when I shake it more chilled than the wine. He is a little jumpy, has been like this perhaps all his life: the only one born outside Liverpool, he had meningitis as a baby, one eye blue, one eye brown 'like David Bowie'. Aged eight, an early smoker, he'd burnt his feet from matches he hid in his socks while he slept. When he was around the same age, Frank had made him and Tony drink a bottle of navy rum after he discovered they'd been steal-ing his. Mick has calmed down since his accident – brain damage from a fight where he hit his head on a kerb. He leaves early to take his tablets. He and Tony have a soft toughness, a tough softness. They remind me of Christopher.

Bernadette, the youngest like our namesake aunty, has my pale, slightly hooded eyes. She talks a mile a minute.

We are all nervous. Bernie is military: 16 years in the army, she served in Iraq. She is funny and fast. She does the speaking and tells the stories. About their dad waking them up when he was back from the pub, playing loud music, having them dance. They adore him. Their mother Irene said they'd put him on a pedestal, and it is noticeable while we talk how mythical he is. The same few phrases and stories return. The pub, the dancing, the drinking, the boxes of chocolates, a warm but remote man in their lives. It is as if they, too, have held on to scraps of cuttings, piecing him together from scant memories. We walk, we eat, we talk, we drink. It is a loud Friday night in Liverpool: thin tops, short skirts, big curlered hair and high heels. A woman holds tight to her friend's shirt trying to walk downstairs on towering shoes. 'We are like elephants,' she says as she eyes me up. She slides down the bannister, skinny skirt around her waist.

There is a rift between the siblings. Bernie and Tony don't talk to Paula and Debbie, though Bernie talks to Donna, who won't talk to Tony. The next morning I meet the big sisters, my second batch of O'Tooles. They look alike. I can see my other sisters in their sadness; something of early Sheila in their shape. It seems Frank had a type.

It is 11am, a December Saturday, we are in our Sunday best. Paula, Donna, Debbie and I. Paula is the eldest. She was a day off 21 when her dad died. Irene died on her fifty-first birthday. She'd been nagging Mick about what to wear when we meet and was concerned about what I'd make of the pub. She wanted him to make a good impression. I tell her I liked the Blob, though not the

Aussie white. I could imagine Frank sat with his mates at the same table night after night, drinking strong wine and navy rum. We walk slowly around 'Paddy's wigwam' – Liverpool's Catholic cathedral of Christ the King. We light candles in the reconciliation chapel. We settle in the refectory and drink tea. We exhume Frank from their memories. They ask about me, I ask about him. We laugh, I choke a little. Irene was 17, Paula says, when they met in her home town. Frank was in his thirties, though he told her he was 21. His children had always thought they had a brother from the photo their mother found in their father's suit. I make it to seven children for both Sheila and Frank. One of 13, like my dad.

Paula and Tony had tried to trace the blond boy to a B&B on the Isle of Man but it was an electrical shop when they found it. The feeling was always there, though, of an older brother in the ether. Our four hours fly. Frank was away a lot and spent most of his time in the pub when at home. Occasionally he would take one of them with him and buy them shrimps (of course), then send them home.

He never said I love you, they say. You couldn't come downstairs in your pyjamas, only fully dressed. They had to leave the room if his friends came. They went to their grandma's once a week. Could only speak if they were spoken to. After Paula moved out, she'd return to make his breakfast every day. It is still raw, the wound he left.

Tony says Paula was more of a mother than Irene. She says he was a naughty boy. But the big sisters won't talk to Tony and Bernadette now. It is not the time to pry.

They walk me to the train, have trouble crossing roads. They are hesitant. It might be my fault. We have a lager in the Lime Street station bar. Frank drank here too. They share photos. Frank as a young man, and later where you can see his life leaving him. Paula gives me his navy papers, a photo with his mates. By the time I get home my stomach's twisted but I got to hear what my father was like as a dad. I stood at his grave and said hello.

I am an iceberg. Most of me is hidden. I feel drained as if I have given blood. It went well with Frank's family. They were gentle and kind. It was almost mundane but now I am flooded like the Lake District. My defences have been breached. My strength is ebbing, my stroke feeble. The shore recedes. I am underwater. Time to float, to trust (if I can), to see where I land.

The next day, I am back at the allotment. It is warm for December. Damp. The tagetes and nasturtiums are lifeless now, unable to hold on. I gather them in my arms. I use just hands. No tools today. I roll them into bundles. Collect them for compost. There is seed where they lay for next spring and summer. I scatter it.

I lift turnips and chioggia, pick parsley and chervil. I buy a chicken on the way home, pack it all in a pot and into the oven for Sunday dinner. I am in need of comfort food.

I am sick of being sad. The useless search for useless family, my elusive peace of mind. Someone once said that kids in care are angry, with no one to draw their rage, like removing venom from a snake. And it was anger that undid my deal with Dudley, corroded my love for Christopher, sometimes still eats me now. And here it is again: intoxicating fury like whisky, stupefying, almost hate.

I wasn't early-wired for rationale, had no adult understanding of my teenage mother, my feckless father, the poverty of love. All I knew was I was on my own, ripped from tit and home.

And here the raging child is grown powerful now. Ready to burn it all out. Obliterate. To call in napalm, to carpet bomb. Like My Lai, like Calley, I am almost eager to lay waste. Time, then, if I can, to limit collateral damage. To stand back from the button.

I will fill a bag with seed. Take a bus. Prepare ground. Lay out string. Sow. And wait for calm. And calendula.

Christopher was mine, my responsibility, as though he was given to me as a kid like he was given his ginger kitten. He was small, hurt, helpless, needing constant care and love. A fearful smile marred by a nervous tic. It worked at first, we curled up together, we whispered reassuring stories. For a long time at least. But like Tuppence we were half wild and I became careless. One day I left Christopher's locked door open and he too slipped away. I wonder would I see him in the right light if I returned to the river? Would he be there, forever six, with his khaki shorts, his bony chest and fishing rod?

I always knew I was more capable than Christopher. Though he was better with his hands and feet, best with boys, I was good with girls, Lilian, Dudley, school. I knew this would matter. I could attract someone to take care of me. I knew that in a war (and I knew that was what it was) it was better to talk yourself out of a fight, no matter how good your fists. I always knew, simply, I was luckier. And in that was everything.

I'd escaped Sheila and her men, scabies, impetigo, herpes, rickets. I'd survived TB. I could talk (and did I talk) and charm and smile. I could make you want me. I was more elastic, stuff didn't stick with me. Though now it sits longer.

The thing with Frank O'Toole has been hard to keep down. I had come to believe I was good at this: tracing Lesley, Ray, Sheila, new brothers and sisters, rediscovering Christopher. I had room for them all. But a lost father was too rich and raw to process. He is still stuck in my throat, undigested. I will be bent out of shape till he is.

The year of the fathers. Of finding Frank, doorstepping Ray, reading Dudley's disturbing thoughts. I didn't discover Francis O'Toole in time. Thirty years is a lifetime late. The young man to a young old man, now a long time dead. I know a little of what a childhood with him was like but the closer I get leaves him further away. I read his navy service records, pore over his pay and identity book. I stare at his sloping signature. I have them both, my mother's and father's now. I have seen their names in their script written before I was born: Sheila's is childlike, less sure of herself; Frank's has an extravagant slope. I have semiology in place of certainty. I read the runes.

Ledger sheet/transfer list
Francis Anthony O'Toole
Ship: Indefatigable: 31.2.52
The rating has it in him to be a good cook but he is indifferent and does not take kindly to authority. It is to be hoped he will do better in new surroundings. He has an engaging personality and I can't help liking him.

The next entry is from two months before me, from HMS *Decoy*, the ship named in Barnardo's. Both my mother's and father's records are written around the same time in the same tone.

> Ship: Decoy 10.11.53
> Professionally he is a good tradesman while in the galleys, and can take charge of Cooks cooking. He cannot take charge of himself and thus is not fit to be a leading hand since by lack of example and weakness about liquor and women outside the ship he is regarded as irresponsible and unclean. I doubt he will ever control his irregularities.

An irregular, unclean father, a morally weak mother, my peculiar legacy.

Later reports write about 'trying to live down his fast reputation'. In June 1956 he passes his professional examination for petty officer with 82 per cent. He is not promoted. By February 1957 he is 'drunk onshore at the Lucky Wheel bar'; in July the same year he is in the ship cells three times in six weeks, bringing on board a bottle of whisky and breaking two windows in the brig.

I hold his youth in my hands, a few sheets of grubby paper, a fading black and white photo. Here he is, stripped to his waist, fists up, pugnacious, a fighting O'Toole, another boxer to add to the family list. Another half-drawn man to be deciphered, his character read from code.

Sickly Ray this year sickened me, half-memories unearthed. More secretive the more he revealed.

So I am left with Dudley, who fostered the differences between my brother and me, who changed my identity, my luck, my life, until he too walked away. The man who sowed my seed.

Is it only people like me, with my past, who obsess over who they are? What, when, where and why? An enigma, nurture or nature? Maybe I am a combination of Frank, Ray, Dudley, all and none of them, a pick-and-mix kid. It is time to stop asking questions, time to be thankful, I think.

A year on the scent of Christopher. Watching his spoor disappear like in snow. I sketch him quickly as he too fades. Close to five years it has taken to see the hole he has left. I have more brothers now, maybe more like him than me, although they don't share his DNA. Closer to the start (wherever, whichever, new beginning that was) Christopher and I were what we had.

The year of the brothers, conjuring Christopher, denying Tony. Teenage Christopher had become an embarrassment. All I could see was his awkwardness, his weakness, his inability to be alone. I won't know what happened with my mother but someone had sucked his marrow before they spat him out.

I could hear his hurt when I was smaller but I lost his frequency. It was there in his need to surround himself with other boys, his dogged devotion to terrible wives. His love lived in baby talk. He had been schooled in his addiction by experts. Groomed and primed to go off when everyone was clear away.

Ravaged by his mother, rejected by his fathers, constantly compared to me. For a while I was his safe place until I, too, traded him. By the time I woke, it was way too late. Now, of course, he is gone for good. I try to retrieve trust but it has been a long lament. My garden journal now a widow's song, I call a loved one lost at sea.

This, then, his eulogy, something spoken at his graveside if he has one, stories collected for the funeral. I carry his coffin. I bear witness. He was my brother. I mourn him still.

My rape and murder dreams are back. I fight them off. I am desperate to breathe, to wake.

It is Christmas again at the Danish summerhouse: wild, windy, still dark, the forecast is for storm, then snow. Here too I grow his marigolds, though I doubt he did again. Not recompense for turning my Judas back but perhaps penance, writing it out repeatedly, like at school.

Sometimes all is over, for the day, all done, all said, all ready for the night, and the day not over, far from over, the night not ready, far, far from ready.
Samuel Beckett, *Happy Days*

Paradise haunts gardens and it haunts mine.

Derek Jarman, *Derek Jarman's Garden*

POSTSCRIPT

Sunday summer afternoon in the other garden in my life, four doors down, where my daughter Kala and her kids Leah and Dylan live. I look out over this space to see them watering the flowers we sow: cosmos, poppies, cornflowers, calendula (of course). I watch as they dead-head the annuals and train their roses, as they thread jasmine through the trellis. I can hear Kala scream as she finds another spider. I see them lying on the grass, sitting and eating and talking with friends.

Kala's garden is a collaboration. I buy too much seed and try to persuade her to let it grow wild, while she and Henri ruthlessly sort it by height and colour. We sow summer annuals on Kala's birthday in May and plant spring tulips in the autumn. It is an urban family flower garden. It is much used and loved.

Today there is a barbecue. Radha, my younger daughter, is first to arrive, with two of her children: Lene and Taylor. Liam, her eldest son, has lived with Henri and me since he was 13. I woke him today at noon, half an hour before everyone is due to arrive. It is his last year as a teenager. Like a cat, he can stay out most of the night and sleep through much of the day. Kala is cooking in her kitchen – jerk chicken, a family favourite. Leah, just back from an Ibizan summer, is preparing her potato salad. Henri and I have brought tomatoes from the terrace, cooked beans and courgettes from the plot.

We are joined by my son Jaime and family: wife Rebecca, Tara and Emily. Tara is four years old, Emily two; both are blonde haired with big blue eyes. It is easy to see myself in them. Immediately, they are swarmed by cousins and aunts, rugs laid on the grass and games laid out, giant wooden noughts and crosses. Dylan and Lene let Tara win. It's a smart and loving move. Emily laughs and claps her hands.

The sun shines, the flowers gleam, there are long hugs and many kisses. Miraculously, we are a tactile family. It has always been important to me.

The barbecue is glowing pleasingly pale. The table is laden with food and jugs and jars.

Taylor is 14 and football mad. He grins and shows off ball-spinning tricks. Everyone is impressed. He has grown tall in the past year. Liam is six foot three. He has been leaning down to hug me for a long time now. He and Taylor huddle together.

Jaime joins me at the barbecue. We grill Kala's chicken. Henri and Radha busily mother around, pouring lemon drinks for the little kids and prosecco for the rest.

Kala's cosmos sway in the slight breeze, ethereal pink. The Mexican sunflowers are covered in bloom. The garden is a little gaudy, like us. Plates are passed and emptied, filled again.

Karen, a photographer friend, takes pictures. It is hard to gather all together except at Christmas. I want always to remember these moments. As I raise a toast, my eyes spill with fresh tears. The family I have been looking for this past year, my whole life, I say, is the one I have with me here.

ACKNOWLEDGEMENTS

First thanks must go to Henriette for her patience and love as I mined deeper into my childhood. To my sisters, Lesley and Susan, for sharing their secrets and for reading the manuscript. To Mary and Howard for their friendship and for sharing Plot 29. To all at Branch Hill. To Louise Haines at 4th Estate for commissioning the book and her encouragement as it grew. To Araminta Whitley at LAW for pithy advice. To Nigel Slater for inspiration. Thanks, too, to some of the people who sheltered me as a child.

PHOTOGRAPHS

p. ix: Summer '59, aged five. Christopher (left) and Alan Jenkins with Lilian Drabble in Aveton Gifford: first day with new clothes, new home, new mum.

p. x (top): Summer '65, aged 11. Peter Drabble's last year at the village school.

p. x (bottom): Autumn equinox '71, aged 17. Peter Jenkins with Hawkwind at the Chalice Well, Glastonbury.

PERMISSIONS

Excerpts from *The Waste Land* by T.S. Eliot, 'Digging' from *Death of a Naturalist* by Seamus Heaney and 'Sunlight' (part I of 'Mossbawn: Two Poems in Dedication') from *North* by Seamus Heaney all reproduced with kind permission from Faber and Faber Ltd.

'I Love The Nightlife' Words and Music by Alicia Bridges and Susan Hutcheson © 1978, reproduced by permission of Sony/ATV Songs LLC, London W1F 9LD.

'Nobody's Child' Words and Music by Cy Coben and Mel Force © 1949, reproduced by permission of Sony/ATV Milene Music, London W1F 9LD.